W9-CEC-645

A Bride's Book of
L·I·S·T·S

···

everything you need to
plan the perfect wedding

marsha heckman

welcome
BOOKS

Published in 2010 by Welcome Books®
An imprint of Welcome Enterprises, Inc.
6 West 18th Street, Suite 4B
New York, NY 10011
(212) 989-3200; Fax (212) 989-3205
www.welcomebooks.com

Text copyright © 2010 Marsha Heckman
Cover photograph copyright © 2010 Richard Jung
Design & Compilation copyright © 2010
by Welcome Enterprises, Inc.

Publisher: Lena Tabori
Project Editor: Gavin O'Connor
Designer: Kristen Sasamoto

All rights reserved. No part of this book may be reproduced
or utilized in any form or by any means, electronic or mechan-
ical, including photocopying, recording, or by any information
storage or retrieval system, without permission in writing
from the publisher.

ISBN: 978-1-59962-091-6
Library of Congress Cataloging-in-Publication data on file.

Printed in China

First Edition

1 2 3 4 5 6 7 8 9 10

For further information about this book please visit online:
www.welcomebooks.com/bridesbookoflists

For further information about *A Bride's Book: An Organizer,
Journal, and Keepsake for the Year of the Wedding*, please visit
online: www.welcomebooks.com/bridesbook

contents

planning ahead

the bride

the ceremony

the reception

the honeymoon

planning ahead

basics

timing

budget

guests, invitations, and registry

the basics

Your wedding—the event where you and your partner declare your love and commitment in front of your community—will be among the most important days of your life and a memory you will hold forever. As if making the all-important decision to marry this person isn't weighty enough, your wedding is likely to be the biggest production you will ever organize.

No one can tell you the best way to get married. I was married with three witnesses in a for-hire chapel, and went to the bowling alley for cheeseburgers afterward. My son had a destination wedding at his bride's family's village in England. My daughter has been married twice, once with just family present in our backyard, and once in a two-centuries-old church on the island of Kauai, with hundreds of guests wearing leis of every color and two pigs roasting in the ground.

Have you always wanted to be the fairy-tale princess bride? Is there a romantic far-away place where you've dreamt of getting married? Do you want to go to Vegas or the county courthouse? Then get ready to organize, research, delegate, and **make lists**. The best results come from breaking down a project into tasks, prioritizing, and then following through. This book will guide you through the many options available, with facts, figures, and lists to help you plan every aspect of your dream wedding.

inspiration

In the months and weeks leading up to your big day, you will likely be obsessed by all things wedding. There are stacks of bridal magazines, hundreds of books, and thousands of websites. You can spend hours watching reality TV wedding shows; my last count was seventeen airing on cable. You can watch several over-the-top big money weddings, destination celebrations, DIY weddings, a series about angry spoiled brides, brides competing to win a honeymoon, brides losing weight. I like the one where a fancy wedding planner makes over the bride and her wedding, too. Some of the most entertaining movies have wedding themes. Rent some and watch with your fiancé or girlfriends, or your mom. The following are some of my favorite wedding-themed movies, magazines, and reality shows.

movies

Betsy's Wedding (1990)

Cousin, Cousine (1975)

Father of the Bride (1950 and 1991)

Four Weddings and a Funeral (1994)

High Society (1956)

Monsoon Wedding (2001)

Muriel's Wedding (1994)

My Best Friend's Wedding (1997)

My Big Fat Greek Wedding (2002)

Philadelphia Story (1940)

Rachel Getting Married (2008)

Runaway Bride (1999)

Steel Magnolias (1989)

True Love (1989)

The Wedding Planner (2001)

The Wedding Singer (1998)

bridal magazines

There are numerous regional wedding magazines that you will find at your newstand which can be very helpful when it comes to identifying local vendors and venues. A few national magazines to check out are:

Bride's ✷ *Modern Bride* ✷ *Martha Stewart Weddings*
Elegant Bride ✷ *InStyle* (wedding edition) ✷ *You & Your Wedding*
Today's Bride ✷ *The Knot* ✷ *Real Simple* (wedding edition)
Contemporary Bride

websites

Look to the web for endless ideas, planning tools, personal wedding website templates, local vendor guides, and bride blogs for sharing experiences and information. New sites are added constantly; it's worth your time to take a look. Here are some great places to get started:

www.theknot.com ✷ *www.brides.com*
www.1weddingsource.com ✷ *www.mywedding.com*
www.weddingwire.com ✷ *www.weddingzone.com*
www.projectwedding.com

(reality) television shows

For fun, but probably not for much actual reality!

Bridezillas (WE) ✷ *My Fair Wedding (WE)*
Platinum Weddings (WE) ✷ *Say Yes to the Dress (TLC)*
Whose Wedding Is It Anyway? (Style)

by the numbers

* Every day, 115,000 couples get married somewhere in the world.
* The city of Istanbul, Turkey, holds the record for the number of weddings in a year with nearly 170,000 weddings in 2009.
* China boasts over 9,000,000 weddings per year, averaging approximately $20,000 each.
* France has the lowest number of marriages per year, less than 1% per capita. However, four times as many unmarried couples are living together compared with twenty years ago.
* Weddings are big business in Japan. There are around 715,000 marriages per year, each with an average cost of $75,000 (more than 25% of Japanese couples marry in Guam to save up to 60% of typical Japanese wedding expenses).
* Ten countries allow marriage of same-sex couples: Belgium, Canada, Holland, Norway, South Africa, Spain, Sweden, Portugal, Iceland, and Argentina.

the american wedding

* 88% of Americans marry at least once.
* The number of weddings every year in the US: over 2.4 million— or 6,575 weddings a day.
* In 1960, an average bride was just 20 years old, her groom 23. Forty years later brides are waiting until they're 27, grooms are now 29 years old.
* Hope springs eternal! One-third of Americans who get married have done it before.
* The average age to get remarried is 34 for women and 37 for men.
* From saying "yes!" to "I do" is usually about 15 months.

the american couple

* The average engaged couple makes $60,000 per year.
* 69% of engaged couples have known each other longer than 3 years.
* 64% of couples live together before marriage.
* More than 4.2 million unmarried couples live together.
* There is a 43% chance of a marriage ending in divorce.

timing

Picking the date is easy for some couples, harder for others. Start with what you have imagined. Have you always dreamed of a garden wedding with roses blooming? Your month is May in most parts of the country. Picturing yourself barefoot on a beach? That's a September wedding, if you live in Northern California. Holiday weekends are popular, but guests may have to pay more for travel and accommodations. If you have a particular venue in mind, check with them right away. A friend who got engaged in February discovered her venue had an open date in April and then nothing until the following spring. She pulled together a wedding in two months rather than wait more than a year!

Weather is a critical factor. That's why "wedding season" is May through October. If you want an outdoor wedding, you can narrow it down again (depending on where you live). Consider how long it takes to put together a wedding, especially if you also work.

Don't forget, the date you choose is one you will celebrate every year for the rest of your life (no pressure)!

Here is an old rhyme for predicting
your future by the month in which you wed:

✳

Married when the year is new,
    he'll be loving, kind and true,
When February birds do mate,
    you wed, nor dread your fate.
If you wed when March winds blow,
    joy and sorrow both you'll know.
Marry in April when you can,
    joy for maiden and for man.
Marry in the month of May,
    you will surely rue the day.
Marry when June roses grow,
    over land and sea you'll go.
Those who in July do wed,
    must labor for their daily bread.
Whoever wed in August be,
    many a change is sure to see.
Marry in September's shrine,
    your living will be rich and fine.
If in October you do marry,
    love will come but riches tarry.
If you wed in bleak November,
    only joys will come, remember.
When December snows fall fast,
    marry and true love will last.

when to marry

tradition and lore

Traditionally, June was the favored month for weddings, and considered to be the luckiest because it is the month of Juno, the goddess of love and marriage.

✻

Summer months were also favored for weddings because men were thought to be more fertile in the summer, and pregnancies resulted in spring births when babies had a better chance of survival.

✻

May was the unluckiest month because it was when the Romans honored Bona Dea, goddess of chastity, and also when they celebrated the Feast of the Dead. Pagans observed the feast of Beltane, the beginning of summer, with orgies and drinking. It was not considered a proper time to begin a marriage.

✻

Weddings held during the Christian tradition of Lent (the 40 days preceding Easter, which usually falls in April) were frowned upon, as it was a time of fasting and abstinence. Queen Victoria actually forbade her children from marrying in May.

An old superstitious Irish rhyme for your choice of day:

Monday for health,
Tuesday for wealth,
Wednesday best of all,
Thursday for losses,
Friday for crosses,
Saturday no luck at all.

✳

Saturday is the most popular day of the week to get married; Sunday a close second. But lately, Friday's becoming the choice of more and more couples who have discovered they can save money, and find more vendors are open for scheduling.

More weddings have become multiple-day affairs, with an average celebration lasting three days. This is particularly true for destination weddings, where the wedding comes between a rehearsal dinner the night before and a brunch the day after.

by the numbers

35% of weddings occur in the summer

29% in the spring

23% in the fall

13% in the winter (11% are Christmas weddings)

✻

53% of weddings occur in the afternoon

31% in the evening, 16% in the morning

✻

December is the most popular month to propose,

beginning one in five engagements.

✻

In the last few years, July was the most popular month for a US
wedding, August was second, and June came in third:

Month:	# of weddings:
January	132,000
February	136,000
March	141,000
April	159,000
May	176,000
June	218,000
July	233,000
August	225,000
September	213,000
October	206,000
November	146,000
December	161,000

take care of yourself

Preparation is one essential key to a less stressful wedding day. Knowing you look and feel your best is the other.

four to two weeks before the wedding

1. Get a physical.
2. See your dentist for a check-up and cleaning. Consider teeth whitening.
3. Get a haircut and color; and practice your wedding day 'do' with your hairdresser. Make your appointments for color touch-up a week before and for the wedding day styling.
4. Hire a make-up artist and have a practice appointment. Or go to a department store and have a makeup demonstration; then buy the products you need to do it yourself.
5. Have a facial.
6. Get a little tan, careful not to burn or spend too long in a tanning booth.

a few days before

1. Get a massage. You could have a spa day with your attendants or your mom.
2. Have a manicure and pedicure.
3. Go to bed early the night before your wedding. You will be excited so it may be hard to do, but you will be happy you did.

budget and cost

American brides spend over $120 billion collectively during the six months before and after their weddings. $72 billion of that number is spent on the wedding itself, with much of the rest on clothes and purchases for the home. While it is traditional for the bride's parents to host and pay for the wedding, it has become increasingly common for the costs to be shared by the two families and the bride and groom.

costs by category

Costs vary from region to region, year to year, and bride to bride. Your own touches and style also affect your budget. Percentages are best to work from; here is an example list that you can tailor to reflect your needs.

Reception: 35%-55%

Ceremony: 6%-10%

Attire: 5%-12%

Flowers: 5%-15%

Entertainment/Music: 3%-10%

Photography/Videography: 7%-13%

Stationery: 2%-3%

Wedding Rings: 3%-7%

Parking/Transportation: 2%-3%

Gifts: 2%-3%

Miscellaneous: 6%-8%

One-third of engaged couples hire a wedding planner. The median fee is 15% of the total cost of the wedding, plus expenses.

10 ways to keep costs down

1. Marry in January, February, March, or November.

2. Marry on a weekday, particularly Friday night.

3. Hold your event at a private club someone in the family belongs to—members get big discounts.

4. Hire a DJ instead of a band. All the songs will sound exactly like you remember them and you'll save a bundle.

5. Instead of high-end rentals, use the standard linens, white or colors, and add a "topper" piece of square sheer fabric to dress them up or add sparkle.

6. Use blooming plants and decorate the containers yourself, or find your local flower market and ask a couple of friends to help you create your own table arrangements.

7. Arrange with the photographer to get your photos digitally or on a disc, and then print them on your own printer or use the photo department at a discount store.

8. Find prom or cocktail dresses in a department store for your bridesmaids.

9. There are *huge* sales on bridal gowns to make room for new designs. Call your favorite bridal store and ask about sale dates.

10. Ask three friends to shoot video as their gift to you. That way nobody feels obligated to do it the whole time. Have one do the ceremony, one do the reception, and one record the guests offering messages to the newlyweds.

by the numbers

The wedding industry brings in $50 billion a year in the US.

*

The average wedding budget is $23,000. The average American wedding costs $28,384. That means a whopping 45% of couples go over budget.

*

The bulk of the budget is the reception venue, including the food (average cost $12,838), followed by a band ($3,288), and video and photography expenses (around $2,500).

*

Approximately 87% of couples have a rehearsal dinner, and nearly a third host a day-after-party, often a brunch with the wedding party and out-of-town guests.

*

When it comes to geography, Arkansas brides spend the least amount of money, averaging just over $15,000 a wedding. It's followed closely by Idaho and Utah.

*

Not so cheap in the Big Apple, where New York City brides spend an average of almost $57,000 on their weddings.

To date, the world's most expensive wedding was a six day affair in France in June of 2004. Steel tycoon Lakshmi Mittal, the fifth richest man in the world, spent more than $60 million on the wedding of his daughter, Vanisha, to Amit Bhatia. What did he spend it on?

* Twelve Boeing jets hired to fly the guests from India to France.
* Printed invitations delivered in silver boxes, containing twenty pages, including romantic poems.
* Bridal *trousseau*, created by top Indian designers Suneet Verma and Tarun Tahiliani.
* Spectacular gold and diamond jewelry for the bride.
* One thousand guests put up in a five-star hotel in Paris.
* An engagement party at the Palace of Versailles.
* A lavish dinner at the Jardin des Tuileries on the right bank of the Seine in Paris.
* Entertainment, including one event featuring can-can girls, à la the Moulin Rouge.
* Ceremony at a 17th century French chateau, Vaux le Vicomte, fifty-five miles from Paris.
* One of the top chefs of Calcutta, flown to Paris to prepare Indian food for the guests.
* Forty-five professional cooks.
* More than ten thousand flowers.
* Unprecedented fireworks displays over the Eiffel Tower.
* Expensive favors for each guest (women received luxurious designer handbags).

guests, invitations, and registry

Once you have decided on a location and date, your next step is creating a guest list and invitations. There are many factors at play here, and the process is potentially fraught with anxiety: Who can be left out? Will feelings be hurt? Was anyone forgotten? Diplomacy and compromise are essential.

guest list

to-do

1. Write down every person in your family and everyone you would invite to your wedding if money, time, and place were absolutely no consideration.

2. Ask your fiancé to do the same.

3. Determine the maximum number of people you can include in addition to yourselves, parents, and wedding party, based on the venue occupancy and/or your budget.

4. Read through both lists and highlight everyone you feel you must have at your wedding.

5. Ask your parents for the names of people they want included on the guest list.

6. How do the numbers compare?

7. Still too many on the list? Establish criteria together for keeping guests on—or off—your final list: Family trumps friends? Friends take precedence over work associates? Out-of-towners over local friends? These are emotionally loaded decisions with important practical applications and must be made thoughtfully. Failing that, flip a coin.

8. Take time to consider the highlighted names and talk it over with each other.

9. You can count on more people to attend a hometown wedding where the couple grew up, less if you go far away for the celebration. Invite 10% more than you expect, to be safe.

10. When you get a "no" response, you can add someone back in.

invitations

The gold standard of invitations comes in an oversize envelope, addressed by hand, with an inside envelope. Traditionally the invitation is heavyweight white or ivory paper, engraved with formal text, and includes a response card with return envelope, and a nice tissue between. Today's options are endless for professionally printed or computer generated designs. Many brides and grooms create their unique invitation themselves, and save-the-date cards, too. Your invitation is the first thing your guests will see to hint at your theme, so put your own stamp on them.

Invitation format:

To single guests:
Mr. Adam B. Jones or Ms. Ann Smith
Address

*

To couples:
Mr. and Mrs. Adam B. Jones
or Mr. Adam Jones and Ms. Marcia Doe
Address

to-do

1. Decide if you need save-the-date cards for faraway guests or for a destination wedding.
2. Order invitations and cards five months before the wedding date. Order 10% more invitations than you need and extra envelopes for mistakes when addressing them.
3. Be certain to carefully proofread invitations. You don't want to misspell your future father-in-law's name.
4. Include printed driving directions.
5. When your list is finalized and your invitations are printed, you may want to hire a calligrapher to address them for you, or gather your bridesmaids to address and assemble them together.
6. Mail invitations six weeks ahead or earlier.
7. Make a designated spot for the response cards and check them against the guests' mailing list.

The average number of guests invited to most weddings: 178. The number who actually attend: 157.

wedding registry

In the early days, a wedding registry was the good memory of the lady who worked in the china section of the town's department store. In the 1920s, one big chain store created the bridal registry to capitalize on the most traditional gift an engaged couple was given: tableware. Every bride selected her favorite china and silver flatware and glassware pattern, and friends and family would buy pieces or place settings. The stores began to keep track to help the bride complete her dinner table. Now couples can register with a huge number of stores for anything they might want or need. There are even several online sites, such as myregistry.com, which allow you to create one registry from multiple stores.

A more recent phenomenon is a cash registry. Couples may set these up for guests to gift money online, or include a wedding wishing well at the reception. The wishing wells (or treasure chests, bird cages, etc.) range from decorated cardboard boxes to wooden constructions and can be designed to match your theme.

Today's wedding guests know they can use your registry to give you a gift you really want; they can select a price and will be the only ones who bought it for you. Or they can choose something else (which you may or may not be able to exchange).

to-do

1. Go to your favorite stores together and shop with the barcode reader gun.

2. Register as many places as you like, but consider what you really need; don't flood people with too many choices. Three to five is a good number of stores.

3. Register online as well as on location at the stores you choose, but don't register on the web exclusively; some people prefer the mall to cyber shopping, and will appreciate the option.

4. Wherever you sign up, be sure to register for items in a range of prices.

5. It feels good to start fresh together with beautiful new bedding and towels. Register at chain department stores and a linens outlet for patterns and colors you both love.

6. Many guests will want their gift to add to your selections of linens and dishes, glassware and flatware. Choose your patterns with your fiancé, and keep in mind they should be classic enough to look good years from now, yet be a true statement about your style as a couple.

6. Final deadline to register is when you mail the invitations.

where to register?

*Think inside your life and outside the box
when you choose the places you want to register:*

Department store
linens, tableware, small appliances, luggage

✻

Home improvement store
materials and tools for the home

✻

Gourmet kitchen store
gourmet cooking utensils and tools

✻

Sporting goods store
sports or camping equipment

✻

Furniture and home stores
accessories for decorating your home

✻

Garden center
plants, trees, lounge furniture,
seeds, gardening tools, and equipment

etiquette

1. Guests eighteen and older should get their own invitation.
2. It is appropriate to invite a single person to bring a guest.
3. If you do not want to include children, tell parents at the time you invite them.
4. Include the names of guests on the inside envelope.
5. It is customary to put a stamp on the response card envelope.
6. *Never* put the stores where you have registered in or with the invitation. Really, *never*.
7. If you have a wedding website, it is acceptable to put your registry information there—and you can put your wedding website on your invitation.

thank you notes

1. Handwritten thank you notes are a requirement when you receive any gift. A phone call or email thank you is not sufficient.
2. Thank you notes should be written within two months after you open the gift. Guests have one year to send you a wedding gift, but your thank you should arrive promptly.
3. Your note should mention the gift specifically and why it was special to you.
4. Thank you letters should include both of your names or signatures.

the bride

dress

accessories

attendants

rings

the dress

For most brides, the dress is the most important personal choice sh
makes for her wedding. You may have been dreaming about th
perfect dress since childhood. It is an essential expression of your pe
sonality and style. The dress sets the tone and degree of formality fo
the entire wedding day. Begin looking early and set a budget. Orde
your dress at least six months ahead.

to-do

1. Cull through bridal magazines and the Internet looking at wedding dresses. Collect pictures of every dress that appeals to you.

2. Make a sketch of the dress you imagine, and write a list of all its desired features.

3. Ask friends to recommend the bridal salon, store, or dressmaker that gave them what they wanted, and with excellent service.

4. Make appointments to try on gowns at two or more stores. Tell them what style you're interested in and what your budget is. Ask them to select some dresses for you in advance. Take your honor attendant and your mother, or a close friend.

5. Wear a strapless bra to try on gowns. If you know what jewelry you will be wearing, bring it with you. Wear shoes with the heel height that is comfortable for you. Bring a camera.

6. Don't be discouraged if you do not find that dream dress in the first store. If you don't find it elsewhere, you could have your dress custom made.

7. Try on several styles of dresses. You may be surprised.

8. Keep all appointments for fittings and get confirmation of the pick-up or delivery date in writing. Be certain the store will press the dress for you and have them put that in writing as well.

9. Make a list of accessories, make up, and lingerie you will need, and shop or order them early to avoid anxiety. Keep everything for the wedding together in one place.

10. Bring your dress home days before the wedding and hang it where it is safe from moisture, dirt, stains, and wrinkles.

favorite designers

Bridal magazines are filled with fantastic full-page color ads for dra-matic designer wedding gowns. You can also view many collections on the designers' websites. Here's a list of favorites to check out:

Monique Lhuillier	Carolina Herrera
Vera Wang	Oscar de la Renta
Lazaro Perez	Amsale Aberra
Reem Acra	Elizabeth Fillmore
Jim Hjelm	Jenny Packham
Peter Langer	Rita Vinieris
Ramona Kereza	Marchesa
Alvina Valenta	

why white?

Sixteenth-century European nobility dictated that white, not blue, would symbolize purity for the bride. At the time, pale or white garments cost more than dark colored ones because bleaching cloth was an expensive process, available only to the affluent. Other symbols of purity worn by more common brides included a coronet of flowers on her head, a veil over her face, her hair down, and orange blossoms or daisies. White as the symbolic color of maidenhood resurfaced in the culture when the virgin Queen Victoria married Albert in a white gown. The trend has changed little since, and in Europe and the United States most brides still wear white.

In Scandinavia, black is a popular choice for the bride's dress. In Ireland green is often worn. In most Asian cultures the bride wears red, the color of luck, joy, and prosperity. A Hopi bride's white dress is woven by the groom and any men in the community who wish to assist him.

Here is a silly Old English rhyme that pairs different dresses with various fates for the bride:

✳

Married in white,
   you've chosen right,
Married in blue,
   your love will be true,
Married in pearl,
   you'll live in a whirl,
Married in brown,
   you will live in the town,
Married in red,
   you'll wish you were dead,
Married in yellow,
   ashamed of your fellow,
Married in green,
   don't want to be seen,
Married in pink,
   your spirit will sink,
Married in grey,
   you'll go far away,
Married in black,
   you want yourself back.

accessories

While your wedding dress is the most important piece of clothing you will ever wear, it is not your entire ensemble. Your lingerie, jewelry, headpiece, a veil, and shoes are all necessities. Once you have settled on your dress, carefully consider what accessories will best enhance the look you are creating and to complement, rather than distract from the beauty of your wedding gown.

"something old, something new"

* "Old" was often a garter given to the bride by a happily married woman or an inherited piece of jewelry. This represents the friends and family you want to keep in your newly married life.

* "New" is usually the bride's dress and embraces the future happiness and prosperity of the couple.

* "Borrowed" should be some small family treasure loaned for the wedding and returned to symbolize both separateness and connection.

* "Blue" in the rhyme may be due to the fact that before Queen Victoria wore a white gown, blue was the most popular dress. "Marry in blue, lover be true," as the saying went. The color blue represents fidelity. In ancient Israel and in Italy brides often wore blue ribbons in their hair on their wedding day. Many brides wear a blue garter, and I've known some who wore blue underwear, blue jewelry, and even blue running shoes.

* "And a sixpence in her shoe," so the bride had a little money of her own. The American version is: "And a lucky penny in her shoe."

the accessories list

1. Headband, tiara, or hair flowers
2. Veil
3. Earrings
4. Brooch
5. Necklace
6. Bracelet
7. Shoes
8. Stockings
9. Garter
10. Bra and panties
11. Gloves
12. Wrap
13. Prayer book, Bible, or rosary
14. Handkerchief
15. Family keepsake

the veil

Brides have been known to wear veils throughout the ages. Wearing a veil would disguise and protect the bride from kidnappers and evil spirits, prevent her from appearing immodest, and keep the groom from seeing her face before taking his vows. Originally worn to deceive or to prevent rejection in an arranged marriage, the veil has lasted through the centuries and is an iconic image of brides.

facts & customs

* In traditional Jewish weddings the groom lifts the veil before the vows to check that he's marrying the woman he expects. In the Bible, Jacob was promised the beautiful Rachel for his wife, but when the veil came off it was her sister, Leah.

* Brides in ancient Rome wore veils.

* In many Asian countries the bride's face is obscured by an elaborate embroidered cloth attached to her headpiece.

* In Muslim and Hindu cultures women cover their faces before and during the ceremony.

* In Mexico and Spain the traditional head covering for brides is the lace Mantilla.

* The "blusher," a veil worn over the bride's face, is not favored by feminists.

wearing a bridal veil

Some brides want that cloud of tulle around her head to be trimmed with ribbon or jewels or lace, and topped with a crown of flowers, or pearl tiara, or a satin headband. Others prefer not to wear one at all. Here are the various options by length:

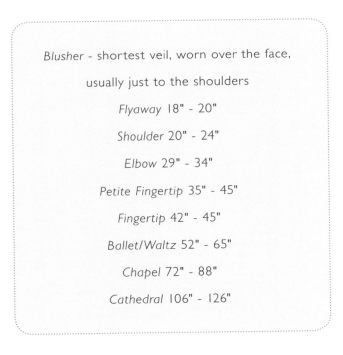

Blusher - shortest veil, worn over the face,

usually just to the shoulders

Flyaway 18" - 20"

Shoulder 20" - 24"

Elbow 29" - 34"

Petite Fingertip 35" - 45"

Fingertip 42" - 45"

Ballet/Waltz 52" - 65"

Chapel 72" - 88"

Cathedral 106" - 126"

shoes

❖❖❖

The bride's shoes should be a perfect pairing with her dress, but comfort along with style should be her guide. Walking down a long aisle, with one hand on her escort's arm, and the other holding her bouquet, all while managing a train and long skirt, is difficult enough. The shoes should be comfortable to avoid stumbles and sore feet from standing in a reception line and an evening of dancing.

tradition and superstition

* For luck, have a house cat eat out of your shoe a week before the wedding.
* For wealth, put a penny (or a sixpence) in your shoe.
* Father gives the groom a pair of his daughter's shoes to symbolize relinquishing his responsibility for her.
* Groom takes the bride's shoe and taps her on the head to let her know who's boss.
* Sometimes groomsmen write a message of luck or encouragement on the bottom of the groom's shoes.
* Bridesmaids sign the soles of the bride's shoes. At the end of the reception whoever's name has worn away is the next to marry.

bridal attendants

The bridal attendants and the groomsmen are there to help and support the two of you before and during the wedding. The groom has a best man or best woman, and the bride must have an "honor attendant." These two sign the license as witnesses to the marriage. Usually there are several other friends and relations to stand up with them in the ceremony. Many couples include a flower girl and a ring bearer in the wedding party.

bridesmaids

The honor attendant is virtually your wedding day lady-in-waiting. She accompanies you to select your dress, hosts your bridal shower, holds the groom's wedding ring, helps you address invitations and make favors, attends all wedding events, and makes a toast at the reception. Bridesmaids throw the bachelorette party, attend all wedding events, go to fittings, assist you in dressing, and help you address invitations and make favors.

Things to consider:

* If you have been an attendant in a friend's wedding, it is customary to return the invitation.

* Don't forget the cute factor! Children add an element that honors the newest generation and represent innocence and purity, bringing luck to the couple. Plus, they are adorable in photos (just don't expect them to always follow instructions)!

* Flower girls and ring bearers are usually under 10 years old. If you do have very young people in your wedding, make sure they make it to the rehearsal!

to-do

1. Choose your sister or best friend to be your honor attendant. Her title is "Maid of Honor" if she's single, and "Matron of Honor" if she's married. If it's a guy you're closest to, he will be your "Man of Honor."

2. Be understanding if you ask someone and she turns you down. There are a lot of duties, and she has to be willing and able to spend time and money and a lot of energy on your wedding. She may want to be a bridesmaid instead, or just a guest.

3. The attendants (or their parents, if they're kids) are responsible for buying their wedding clothes. If you know this is a hardship, you may decide to pay for dresses and shoes yourself. Alternatively you could ask for a more general dress code, such as, "wear something blue."

4. The bride is expected to give her attendants a thank-you gift. Often this is the jewelry worn with their bridesmaid dresses at the wedding. It is thoughtful to pick up similar styles but different pieces for each woman. Who wants the exact same earrings as four of your friends, unless they're diamonds? Make your choice genuinely personal for each of them.

The average size of a wedding party is 12.

gift list

1. Jewelry with each one's birthstone (*see page 63*)
2. A keepsake locket engraved with the wedding date and he initials.
3. Silver frame with a note that it will be filled with her portrai from the wedding photographer.
4. Anything from Tiffany. They have sterling-silver key chain under $100.
5. Charm bracelet with a charm chosen just for her, and one as a reminder of the wedding.
6. Monogrammed makeup compact.
7. Luxurious spa robe with monogram.
8. Jewelry box or music box.
9. Tickets for a concert, ballet, stage show.
10. Professional sports event tickets.
11. Cute pajamas & slippers.
12. Designer scarf or pashmina.
13. A beautiful photography book on a subject she loves, or her favorite romantic poetry.
14. Gift baskets: bath & beauty products; hair care products; gour met cooking items and cookbook; picnic basket with dishes glasses, and good wine, cheese, and fruit. Pack each basket with a theme just for her in mind.
15. Gift certificates: favorite clothing store, makeup and makeup demonstration, facial, mani/pedi, massage, spa day, or high end restaurant.

tradition and lore

In the Western tradition, the practice of surrounding the bride with similarly dressed young women started as a defense against the bride-stealing Anglo-Saxon and Germanic marauders. The earliest bridesmaids often dressed identically to the bride, in the same color gowns—including veils—to act as decoys and confuse potential kidnappers.

✳

It was also once believed that surrounding the bride with a flock of bridesmaids would ward off harmful spirits who might place a curse on the bride and groom's happiness. Early Greek maidens often wed at age fifteen, and tradition called for these young brides to be escorted by a train of happily married, fertile women who served the dual purpose of protecting the bride from evil and allowing their own good fortune to rub off on her.

✳

In some cases, bridal parties took extreme measures, dressing like men to protect themselves against misfortune. In Denmark, the bride and groom changed sex roles to ensure a successful wedding. One ancient Jewish tradition called for the bride to be clad in full armor, complete with helmet and weaponry.

What of the groom's best man? In days of yore, he was generally the right-hand man of the thieving tribesman, ready to assist in snatching the "bride elect." Additional comrades ensured a successful raid and, if they were lucky, might steal a bride of their own.

the bridal shower

In the past a groom could expect a dowry to sweeten the deal when he bargained for his bride. But if the family didn't have money or the marriage wasn't approved, a woman would not have a dowry or *trousseau*. The female friends of the prospective bride would come to her house and "shower" her with household items so she didn't come to her husband empty-handed.

✳

In the 1950s bridal showers were very in vogue, with fancy sandwiches, cake, ice cream sherbet with champagne punch, cutesy wedding bell decorations, and silly games. The current trend in showers includes male friends and family members at an evening party, or a Sunday barbeque. My son and his bride-to-be had a barbeque and touch-football game *and* opened presents. The gifts are still for the couple's home unless the theme calls for specifics.

1. Usually the maid/matron of honor hosts the bridal shower.

2. Food and drink should be offered, but it isn't necessary to have a whole meal.

3. The bridal shower is often a surprise for the bride. Someone should be responsible to get her there without giving away the secret.

4. Be sure to take pictures and give the bride prints or email them to her.

5. Invitations should go to family and friends and the wedding attendants. They can be very casual—mailed, emailed, or phoned.

6. Do not ask people who are not invited to the wedding, it's just plain greedy. The exception is work showers. Co-workers may want to throw you a separate shower, even if they are not on the wedding guest list.

7. While you open presents, make sure someone takes all the ribbons from the gifts and makes you a bow-bouquet for the rehearsal.

8. Assign someone to write down the gifts and who brought them. You will be grateful for this list when writing your thank-you notes.

Trousseau: Old French term for the "little bundle" of linens the bride would bring to her marriage. Now it means the new outfits the bride buys for all of the wedding activities, the lingerie under her wedding gown, and her wedding-night clothes.

shower themes

❋ **Clock shower:** Starting with 6 a.m., assign guests a time and ask them to bring a gift that is for that time of day (coffee maker for morning times, cooking items for meal times, bed linens for night hours). Have the guest of honor open them in order for a whole day of presents.

❋ **Gourmet shower:** Invite guests to bring cooking gifts and a favorite recipe to give to the couple. Hire a chef to give a demonstration and prepare some of the food you serve.

❋ **Flower shower:** Hold a garden party, and hire a florist to do a flower-arranging class. Provide flowers for each guest to make her own arrangement. Have guests bring their own small container for their take-home bouquet.

❋ **Lingerie shower:** Invitations should include the bride's sizes—bra, panties, and nightgown. Provide note cards and have each guest write down advice to her about marriage and lovemaking.

❋ **Bed and bath shower:** Organize a spa trip or hire a masseuse to give foot rubs, paint one another's nails, and watch a great wedding movie. Everyone wears jammies and robes and brings presents for the bath or bedroom.

❋ **Honeymoon shower:** If the couple already have everything they need for their home, create the atmosphere of their destination, have food befitting the location, foreign currency, neck pillows, or anything that's for fun and luxury during their trip.

❋ **Afternoon tea:** Serve finger sandwiches, scones, petit fours and of course, tea! This one is a classic tradition, and it is suitable for both your girlfriends and older relatives and in-laws. Tell the guests to wear hats and gloves.

shower games

Party games—while they can be silly and embarrassing—are great icebreakers and can make a group bond and laugh together.

* **The bride and I:** Guests bring a small token that represents how they know the bride. The tokens are all put in a box. The bride-to-be pulls them out one at a time and guesses who brought what. Between them, the story of how they met is told, and everyone knows a bit about everyone else.

* **Something blue:** Everyone brings something blue for the bride. The guest of honor is blindfolded, feels the item, guesses what it is and why someone would give it to her. The guests who brought gifts she could not identify win prizes.

* **Gift bingo:** The hostess provides blank bingo cards. Before the bride-to-be begins opening gifts, each guest fills the squares of her card with guesses of what the presents will be. As each gift is opened, guests mark off a square if they predicted it. First to mark five guesses in a row wins.

* **TP gown:** This is hilarious after a few mimosas. You need tape, scissors, and a LOT of toilet paper. Guests make teams of 3 or 4. One is the model; the others make a bridal ensemble using only toilet paper and tape on her. Have a fashion show with the bride choosing the winning team.

the bachelorette party

The bachelorette party is a descendent of the English and Irish "stag-ette" or "hen party." The bride-to-be and the women closest to her would get together for an evening of "girl talk" before the wedding. The women passed on their wisdom about marriage and shared secrets, often about sex, with the guest of honor.

As an example of women's sexual freedom and equality, the modern bachelorette party became increasingly popular in the 1990s. Today more than 90% of brides have bachelorette parties the week before the wedding.

Smaller than the bridal shower, the bachelorette party is usually a night out for the close girlfriends of the bride, planned and hosted by the bridesmaids. Although this party is not given by the bride, she should have input in the planning:

1. Ask the hostesses what activities are being planned; there are some things you may not wish to do.

2. Provide the hostesses with a guest list that includes all the adult bridal attendants, plus any other very close girlfriends you want to come. It is perfectly acceptable for anyone to decline, as it isn't a traditional duty. Never ask someone who was not invited to the wedding.

3. The participants may agree to contribute to the cost of the activities, but the bride does not.

party ideas

As fancy as a weekend getaway or as simple as a brunch in your back-yard, there are many ways to have a bachelorette party:

* **Weekend away:** Head to a vacation home or hotel to relax and swim, ski, or whatever strikes you as a fun getaway for "the girls" before the wedding.

* **Spa day (or night):** The group takes over a nail salon or spa for facials and massage. You can also hire manicurists to come to your house or hotel to give everyone a mani/pedi.

* **Night out:** Dinner, followed by bar or club-hopping (including a strip club) for cocktails and maybe a little decadence. Hire a limo and bring champagne to make toasts along the way.

* **Restaurant or hotel suite party:** Food and drinks, a slideshow of old photos of the bride-to-be and friends, and hired entertainment. One out of five bachelorette parties hire strippers.

* **Brunch or luncheon:** An alternative to the night out. Hold it at a friend's home or a private room at a restaurant, and enjoy the company of the women in her life together.

Mehndi night is a North African and Middle Eastern party for the women on the night before the wedding. While friends and family celebrate, the bride's hands and feet are decorated with delicate symbolic patterns painted in henna.

wedding day emergency kit

———— ⬦⬦⬦ ————

This is a good assignment for your honor attendant. Make a kit with everything you may need to handle a grooming or dress emergency.

1. Tissues
2. Touch up cosmetics
3. Comb & brush
4. Hairspray
5. Eye drops
6. Band-Aids
7. Safety pins
8. Double-sided tape *(for dress slippage or ripped hem)*
9. Needle and thread *(match the bridal gown and attendants' dresses)*
10. Clear nail polish
11. Emery board
12. Extra stockings
13. Ice pack *(get one you squeeze to activate)*
14. Cough drops
15. Aspirin or other pain reliever
16. Breath mints
17. Baby wipes *(great for makeup stains)*
18. Cornstarch or baby powder *(to cover a stain on white fabric)*
19. Feminine hygiene products

rings

Your wedding ring is the outward sign of your marriage commitment. This is the most important piece of jewelry you will ever have. Will you be wearing a family heirloom, shopping jewelry stores, or designing your own?

Both you and your groom should be comfortable with how the rings feel, and enjoy how they look on your hands. Choose with your heart—you will wear it for many years, and perhaps someday hand it down to your children.

choosing the rings

———— ✧✧✧ ————

Begin your search for rings no later than two or three months before the wedding, since you may need extra time to order, re-size, or engrave them. Determine the proper size for your rings late in the day, not after you have just exercised, and when your body temperature is normal. Fingers swell overnight, when you work out, and when you are hot, and they shrink when you are cold. If you're working with a vintage ring, you may want a jeweler to resize it for you. Help narrow the choices to the perfect one by making some decisions before you shop:

1. What is your budget?
2. Matching or different bands?
3. Gold (14K, 18K, or 24K, the gold content makes a difference in the depth of the color), white metal (white gold, platinum, silver), or a combination?
4. Plain design or ornate?
5. Antique or new?
6. Gems or no gems?
7. Buy or have them custom made?
8. Engraved on the inside?
9. What to engrave: date, initials, sentiment?

buying the rings

After you answer the pre-shopping questions together, you can start looking for your rings:

1. Notice the rings friends and family wear. If you see one you like, investigate.

2. Look in bridal magazines for ideas and fresh designs for simple wedding bands and creative and unusual rings.

3. Browse. Try on lots of rings. Tell the salesperson your budget and preferences; or he/she will show you rings that fit your price range.

4. If you'd like your wedding ring to have colored stones, consider the gem representing the month of your wedding or one or both of your birthstones.

5. Be sure your ring fits with your engagement ring; the jeweler can make adjustments.

6. There should be two or more marks stamped into the metal on the inside shank of the band. One is the manufacturer's mark and the other is the quality mark of the metal. If it is platinum it will say "Plat," if gold, the karat weight (e.g., 24K).

7. Jewelers should give you a certificate of a professional gemologist's "grading report" from an established gem society, for any diamonds you buy.

8. Give yourself at least 24 hours to think over your final choice before buying.

care for your rings

1. Take a close-up photo of your rings in case you ever need to replace them.
2. After you buy the rings, insure them against loss and theft.
3. Polish metal rings with a soft cloth, clean them with toothpaste.
4. Chlorine can pit metal and degrade the setting prongs, so avoid repeated exposure.
5. Leave your rings at home when doing very active sports or working with high heat or power tools.
6. If you regularly take your rings off, you have much less chance of losing them if you make a particular place to put them—and *always* put them there. (Pockets and the sink are *not* good places to put rings.)

Not all engagements mean diamonds, but most do. 75% of first-time brides and 67% of repeat brides will receive a diamond engagement ring.

choosing a colored stone

Although the western origin of birthstones goes back to Moses, in 1912 the American National Retailers Jewelers Association approved a modern birthstone list for purely commercial purposes. Below is the current list of month/gem pairings, as well as a list based on the zodiac.

modern birthstones

January—*garnett*

February—*amethyst*

March—*aquamarine*

April—*diamond*

May—*emerald*

June—*pearl, moonstone*

July—*ruby*

August—*peridot, sardonyx*

September—*blue sapphire*

October—*opal, pink tourmaline*

November—*topaz, citrine*

December—*turquoise, zircon*

zodiac sign birthstones

Aries—*ruby, jasper*

Taurus—*emerald, golden topaz*

Gemini—*pearl*

Cancer—*red coral*

Leo—*green jade*

Virgo—*yellow sapphire*

Libra—*diamond*

Scorpio—*blue sapphire*

Sagittarius—*amethyst*

Capricorn—*beryl, smoky quartz*

Aquarius—*blue sapphire*

Pisces—*jade, aquamarine*

the ceremony

location

vows and readings

superstition

music

location

Choosing the right location site and venue for your wedding is the first decision you make in the planning process. Even the date can depend on where you have your celebration. Many couples will marry in their own church, temple, or mosque and hold the reception in a separate venue.

to-do

Review sites in your local area online. Websites like www.herecomes-theguide.com are a valuable tool that can give you information on capacity, catering, amenities such as furniture and parking, and fees. Sit down with your fiancé and parents and discuss where to have your wedding. Consider the following:

1. Do you want to be married at home?
2. Intimate or the more the merrier?
3. Indoors or outside?
4. Daytime or evening event?
5. Formal or informal?
6. Same ceremony & reception site or separate locations?
7. What kind of location works well for your theme?
8. Do any of you belong to a private club with banquet facilities? Is it a place you like?

80% of traditional (religious) weddings are performed in a church or synagogue.

where to marry?

* **Home:** Yours, your parents', or a friend's is a familiar place where you feel comfortable, and it's free. The size of the house and garden space will determine the number of guests you may include. Remember you will need to rent tables and chairs as well as place settings and linens.

* **Clubs:** Waterside, on the golf course, or in a city mansion can be beautiful settings for photos. They provide activities for the guests—such as golf, tennis, and boating. The food may not be the best, however, and the members may be on-site while your event is going on.

* **Banquet hall:** Usually the staff is highly experienced and efficient. They offer packages, but they often have several bookings on the same day. They can be pushy about their way of doing things, and may be reluctant to make changes or special accommodations for you.

* **Resort or hotel:** Can have an appealing ambiance or may need a magic touch to transform the room. Plenty of amenities for out-of-town guests, easy transportation to and from the airport, and often a hotel will give you a suite in which to get ready, and a free room for the wedding night.

* **Restaurant:** The advantage of a restaurant reception is that the food can be fabulous. If you have a theme, a restaurant can already have the décor and atmosphere you want. The number of guests could be an issue, and there may not be room for dancing. You can use the banquet room or buy out the restaurant for the event.

* **Historic mansion:** Both indoor and outdoor spaces, beautiful architecture, memorable for its history and ambiance, and your party will be the only renter that day. These locations can be expensive, but you spend less on decorating.

* **Museum, aquarium, library:** This is different from a hall or club because the place becomes the theme, and the surroundings are entertaining and cultural. Some have experienced event coordinators; some require dealing with a government agency with lots of red tape, limitations, and rules. It is expensive, dramatic, and unforgettable.

* **Public park, garden, beach:** Nature provides the beautiful and casual setting, but the city must grant you a permit, you may not have privacy, there are lots of restrictions, and you have to bring everything: tables and chairs, place settings, dance floor, electricity, cooking equipment, portable restrooms. You have to deal with dirt, noise, bugs, and weather. Outdoor weddings must have a backup plan for bad weather.

photography

You have chosen your photographer for the quality and style of his or her wedding portfolio. Describe what you like about their work and how you'd like your photos to reflect those qualities. You might start with an engagement portrait of you both, or a bridal portrait at the studio. Consider having some of the pictures taken in black and white as well as color. You will want posed, formal setups as well as candid shots of the festivities and the guests. You may also want them to shoot the rehearsal dinner the night before or the brunch on the following day. Make sure you negotiate how your pictures will be delivered. Will the photographer provide proof prints or an online gallery for you to chose from? Are a specific number of prints included, or do some cost extra? Can he or she give you a CD with your photos so you can print them yourself? And, make sure you give your photographer a list of "don't miss" shots:

photo checklist

Before the wedding:

* Bride/Groom getting ready
* Bride and parents/escort
* Bride and attendants
* Groom and parents
* Groom and best man/ groomsmen
* Leaving for ceremony
* Arrival at ceremony

Ceremony:

* Wedding party entrances
* Bride and escort walking down aisle
* Exchanging vows and rings
* The kiss
* Wedding party exiting
* Bride with bridesmaids
* Groom with groomsen
* Bride/Groom with family
* Formal poses

Reception:

* Exterior
* Reception line
* Bride and groom's entrance
* Cake/cake cutting
* Head table
* Guest tables
* Speeches and toasts
* First dance
* Bride and father dancing
* Groom and mother dancing
* Various dancing
* Bouquet throw/catch
* Garter throw
* Bride and groom's exit

destination weddings

Every year the number of couples deciding to have their wedding away from home grows. For second marriages the figure is 60%. You two may choose a location that has special meaning or wonderful memories, your favorite sport activities (diving, skiing, river rafting, or baseball spring training), or it could be a place you've heard about and long to visit. Perhaps you want the fun of being away with family and friends for this celebration. A destination can fulfill a dream or fantasy on this important occasion, and create a wonderful bond of experience with the people who come. You might think a destination wedding would be more expensive than one in your hometown, but there is almost always a far smaller number of guests, so it can cost a lot less. In Mexico or the Caribbean you could save as much as 75% over a New York or Los Angeles wedding.

16% of all weddings are destination weddings and the number is growing fast (it goes up about 10% a year!).

five top wedding destinations: north america

Las Vegas (100,000 weddings/year)
Hawaii (25,000 wedding/year)
Bahamas (5,000 weddings/year)
Jamaica (5,000 weddings/year)
US Virgin Islands (4,000 weddings/year)

five top beach wedding destinations

Cancun, Mexico
Mount Desert Island, Maine
Cape Breton, Nova Scotia
Vancouver Island, British Columbia
Saint Thomas, US Virgin Islands

ten popular american locations to consider

Central Park, New York City, NY
Chapel of Love, Bloomington, MN
Columbia Gorge Hotel, Hood River, OR
Disneyland, Anaheim, CA
Empire State Building, New York City, NY
Graceland Wedding Chapel, Las Vegas, NV
Little Church of the West, Las Vegas, NV
The Palace of Fine Arts, San Francisco, CA
Philadelphia Zoo, Philadelphia, PA
Westin Beach Resort, Key Largo, FL

to-do

1. List the places and locations that interest you for your celebration.

2. List all the people you know you *must* include in your plans. Decide if this includes children.

3. Make note of difficulties anyone on your list may have traveling to the locations. Consider:
   · long flights
   · extreme weather, humidity, and altitude
   · accessibility (stairs and climbing, walking vs. transportation, access to medical care)
   · services for children
   · ability to afford the trip*

4. Decide who you want in your wedding party. Ask them if they will be able to come.

5. Research venues in the place you like online or at the library. Then email or phone the hotels or resorts to be sure you have up to date information. Ask about using their wedding coordinator, availability on the dates you want, and prices for hotel rooms, ceremony and reception locations, and a per-person estimate for food and drink.

* A destination wedding is a big financial commitment for guests. If you can, you may wish to reduce their expenses by arranging to pay for meals, rooms, and/or transportation.

6. If your parents are paying all or part of the wedding costs, now is the time to bring them in on the decision. Multiply the number of family members and/or friends you will be treating by the cost of the transportation per person. Add the cost of hotel rooms for those same people. Then add the estimated costs for the wedding, the reception, and the rehearsal dinner (which should include all guests). This gives you an idea of the minimum you'll need to spend.

7. Find out the local legal requirements for marriage: fee, residency, waiting period, blood tests or health certificate, witness requirements, and what documents are needed. Some countries have little to no requirements, perhaps not even a license. Others have more complicated requirements that should be taken care of as early as you can.

8. When you determine which place is workable, affordable, and your favorite, make the reservations. You may want to bring in a travel agent to handle booking the transportation and provide coordination for booking hotel reservations. The small additional cost is well worth the time, effort, and stress you save yourself.

9. Communicate with the concierge or wedding coordinator at the location. Get a complete description of services to be provided by them, and any additional costs. Confirm in writing. They can help you figure out extras like flowers, cake, officiate, band, etc.

10. Decision made, prepare and send the "Save the Date" cards about six months ahead.

destination duties

1. Bride and groom are the hosts, joining all scheduled events, making sure everyone is involved and comfortable. It's their job to have fun and get married.

2. Bride's attendants give a bridal shower and often a bachelorette party. These events should include only those who will be attending the wedding; it is considered rude for someone to be asked to give a gift when they aren't attending.

3. The attendants keep track of the groom's ring and the bride's luggage, bridal accessories, and dress at all times. They stay with the bride and help make things easy for her on her wedding day.

4. Groomsmen throw a bachelor party for the groom, which may be before the journey, or at the location. They keep track of the bride's wedding ring and the groom's wedding attire.

5. Bride's parents may be paying for the bulk of a wedding; traditionally they finance the ceremony, the reception, and the bride's outfit, but should not feel obligated to pay for guests' transportation. If the bride and groom are sharing the cost, they may take care of expenses for the wedding party, the events for the guests, and hotel accommodations.

6. Groom's parents pay their own expenses, and traditionally host and pay for the rehearsal dinner.

7. Guests pay their own expenses for a destination wedding, except food at the scheduled events. Guests give a wedding gift, but they should send them to the bride's home before or after the wedding trip.

feeling extravagant?

Ten of the most gorgeous and exotic places in the world to marry:

* **Four Seasons Hotel George V** (Paris, France): Paris is the City of Lights and this hotel is in the heart of it all. Splurge on catering by the hotel's 2-Michelin-star restaurant and indulge in the opulent beauty of its banquet halls, with your photos taken on the Grand Staircase.

* **Positano, Italy** (Amalfi Coast): This storybook little town clings vertically to the Amalfi coast. Get married on the terrace of the town hall with gorgeous views of the water and follow with a reception at any one of the many romantic hotels within walking distance.

* **Le Saint Géran** (Mauritius, Indian Ocean): Island vibe with Asian and African cultural elements and pristine white sand beaches, perfect for a barefoot wedding. This Mauritius five-star resort hotel has private villas, a luxury spa, and Gary Player–designed golf course. It makes an unforgettable destination. You can go on safari for your honeymoon from here.

Hawaii has the most casual weddings (think barefoot on the beach!), while New Jersey and Long Island host the most black tie-events.

* **Cathedral Peak Hotel** (Drakensberg, South Africa): See bush men's ancient rock paintings, waterfalls and gorges; ride horses, play golf, hike and swim in luxury accommodations. Marry here in May to see African big game; the view from the stone and thatch wedding chapel is spectacular.

* **Tandjung Sari Resort** (Sanur, Bali): You can book all twenty-six bungalows at this tiny family-owned boutique resort. Each bungalow is different, the ocean views are beautiful, and the hotel's beach is a lovely site for you ceremony. The food in Bali is delicious.

* **Dalhousie Castle** (Edinburgh, Scotland): The ultimate princess fantasy demands a castle for her nuptials. This thirteenth century Scottish castle is now a luxury hotel with twenty-seven elegant bedrooms, many of them decorated in historical themes. Their Dungeon Restaurant is a favorite for rehearsal dinners.

* **Palace of the Legion of Honor** (San Francisco, CA): Say your vows in front of a glass pyramid and Rodin's Thinker, dance in view of the Golden Gate Bridge and amazing views of the entrance to San Francisco Bay. This neo-classical art museum by the sea is a beautiful building; weddings under a tent in the entrance-courtyard or the lawn in front are unforgettable.

* **California wine country** (Napa County): Have a sit-down dinner in a wine cave, marry in an old stone church, and ride to the reception in horse & buggy. There are sites to rent from palace to hilltop vineyard. Enjoy the finest wines and gourmet dining from world-renowned chefs in a vineyard under a tent or the courtyard of a famed winery.

- **Grand Hyatt** (Poipu, Kauai, HI): Acres of peaceful hidden gardens, white sand beach, spectacular fresh and salt water swimming pools, surfing, kayaking, and luaus are all available. The wedding can take place in a garden gazebo on a grass knoll overlooking the blue Pacific, with a vivid sunset as your background.

- **Wave Hill** (Bronx, NY): Just a stone's throw north of the Big Apple, this mansion on the Hudson has become host to some of New York City's most luxurious weddings. Its extensive formal gardens and pergola, with a backdrop of the river and the Palisades beyond, make for memorable photographs.

f you're not from Nevada, Las Vegas is a destination wedding! The wedding capital of the US, Las Vegas hosts more than 100,000 weddings a year. It's a town that caters to gamblers and couples getting married. There is no residency requirement in Nevada, so impromptu weddings take place within minutes of arrival. Wedding "chapels" have convenient package deals, too: order just the ceremony, or everything from flowers and rings to music, video, and photographs.

vows and readings

Your vows, whether modern, religious, or uniquely personal, are the binding promises you and your groom make to each other. They are the expression of the significance you have, and will have forever, in each other's lives. Take some time to find the perfect vows for each other, or write these promises and the truth about your feelings for your partner yourselves.

If you want to have someone close to you read a poem or other writing about love and marriage during your ceremony, here are a variety of traditional and modern readings that may appeal to you and the reader both. While you may leave the decision to your individual readers, you should also explore the many wonderful expressions of love and marriage that may be recited during your ceremony.

who marries you?

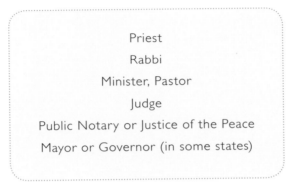

Priest

Rabbi

Minister, Pastor

Judge

Public Notary or Justice of the Peace

Mayor or Governor (in some states)

* Your dear friend or relative can obtain a ministry license online (the oldest and most well-known source is Universal Life Church) and legally marry you.

* In Massachusetts and California anyone can get a one-day permit to perform a wedding.

* Texas and New York allow clergy and a long list of public officials.

* Minnesota authorizes representatives of Native American tribes.

* In Colorado and Wisconsin you can officiate at your own ceremony.

* Ship's captains never had authority to perform marriages, unless they were also clergy. It's a myth perpetrated by old movies and romance novels.

VOWS

religious

If you marry in a church you will take the customary vows according i your religion. You may add to these your own vows, and speak the afterward, if you like. Jewish, Catholic, Episcopal, Methodist, Luthera Presbyterian and Baptist marriage ceremonies have very nearly th same language for the vows made aloud by the bride and groor Making these familiar vows are promises to each other:

* To love, honor, comfort, cherish, and be faithful only to eac other until death.
* To keep these vows whether sick or well, rich or poor.
* To maintain a union in front of God and the religious commu nity, and ask that your marriage be sanctioned by them.

secular

If you have a nonreligious or secular ceremony, and want to find the perfect vows for you, the Internet is a treasure trove. Here are some suggested sites:

www.elegantweddingvows.com ✶ www.weddinggoddess.com
www.weddingyellowpages.net ✶ www.keepandshare.com
www.weddingvowsden.com

write your own

If you wish to write your own vows, start making notes now—don't wait 'til the night before the ceremony. Those words, spoken from your heart, are the most meaningful of all.

1. How did your life change from your meeting?
2. When / how did you realize this is the *one*?
3. Make a list of everything you want to promise.
4. Write freely, edit later.
5. Add a special quote, song lyric or poem with shared meaning.
6. Read your list out loud, then edit it down to what you want to say.
7. Type or write clearly on good paper with tear-proof ink.
8. Practice with your mom or honor attendant.

You'll also find many wonderful ideas for vows and readings in the following books:

* *Complete Book of Wedding Vows: Hundreds of Ways to Say "I Do"* by Diane Warner
* *Complete Book of Christian Wedding Vows, The Importance of How You Say "I Do"* by H. Norman Wright
* *I Do! I Do! The Marriage Vow Workbook* by Shonnie Lavender & Bruce Mulkey
* *The Wedding Ceremony Planner: The Essential Guide to the Most Important Part of Your Wedding Day* by Judith Johnson
* *Weddings from the Heart: Contemporary and Traditional Ceremonies for an Unforgettable Wedding* by Daphne Rose Kingma

readings

religious

"But at the beginning of creation God made them male and female. For this reason a man will leave his father and mother and be united to his wife, and the two will become one flesh. So they are no longer two, but one. Therefore what God has joined together, let man not separate."

—Mark 10:6-9

More suggested readings:

* *"For love is as strong as death…"* —Song of Songs 2:8-10, 16a; 8:6-7a

* *"Two are better than one…"* —Ecclesiastes 4:9-12:9

* *"It is not good for the man to be alone."* —Genesis 2:18-24

* *"There is no fear where love exists…"* —John 4:18

* *"Blessed is every one who…walks in His ways."* —Psalm 128:1-4

* *"Lord, make me an instrument of your peace…"* —The Wedding Prayer by St. Francis of Assisi

* The Seven Blessings —from *The New Jewish Wedding* by Anita Diamant

modern

Understand, I'll slip quietly
Away from the noisy crowd
When I see the pale
Stars rising, blooming, over the oaks.

I'll pursue solitary pathways
Through the pale twilit meadows,
With only this one dream:
You come too.

—Rainer Maria Rilke

More suggested readings:

* *"Because to the depths of me, I long to love one person..."*
  from *Why Marriage?* by Mari Nichols-Haining
* "All I Want" by Renée Duvall
* "Love Is Friendship Caught Fire" by Laura Hendricks
* "With You by My Side" by René Duvall

romantic

You have become mine forever.
Yes, we have become partners.
I have become yours.
Hereafter, I cannot live without you.
Do not live without me.
Let us share the joys.
We are word and meaning, unite.
You are thought and I am sound.
May the nights be honey-sweet for us.
May the mornings be honey-sweet for us.

—Hindu Marriage Poem

More suggested readings:

* "My Love" by Linda Lee Elrod
* "Dance Me to the End of Love," lyrics by Leonard Cohen
* "On Love" by Khalil Gibran
* "Looking For Your Face" by Rumi
* "Love" by Roy Croft

inspirational

Man and woman are like the earth, that brings forth flowers
    in summer, and love, but underneath is rock.
Older than flowers, older than ferns,...
    older than plasm altogether is the soul underneath.
And when, throughout all the wild chaos of love slowly a gem forms,
    in the ancient, once-more-molten rocks of two human hearts,
    two ancient rocks, a man's heart and a woman's,
    that is the crystal of peace,
    the slow hard jewel of trust,
    the sapphire of fidelity.
The gem of mutual peace emerging from the wild chaos of love.

    —"Fidelity" by Dorothy Colgan

More suggested readings:

* "Touched by an Angel" by Maya Angelou
* "Now you will feel no rain, for each of you will be the shelter..."
    —Apache Wedding Blessing
* "May your mornings bring joy and your evenings bring peace."
    —Celtic Wedding Blessing
* "Foundations of Marriage" by Regina Hill
* "On Love" by Thomas Kempis

spiritual

Creator in heaven above
    please protect the ones we love.
We honor all you created as we pledge
    our hearts and lives together.
We honor mother-earth
    and ask for our marriage to be abundant
    and grow stronger through the seasons;
We honor fire and ask that our union be warm
    and glowing with love in our hearts;
We honor wind and ask we sail though life
    safe and calm as in our father's arms;
We honor water to clean and soothe our relationship
    that it may never thirsts for love;
With all the forces of the universe you created,
    we pray for harmony and true happiness
    as we forever grow young together.
Amen

—Cherokee Wedding Prayer

More suggested readings:

✽ "On Marriage" by Kahlil Gibran

✽ "Wedding Prayer" by Robert Louis Stevenson

✽ *"May the road rise up to meet you"* —Traditional Irish Blessing

✽ "Prayer for Kindness" by the Bahá'u'lláh

✽ "On Love" from *A History of Love* by Diane Ackerman

superstitions

Every civilization has a marriage ceremony. The community gathers to witness and support the joining of a couple. All cultures have traditions, customs, and superstitions that have been woven into the fabric of their societies over time. As the community gathers to witness and support the joining of a couple, ancient customs are included to enhance and protect the union.

superstitions

If she knows what to do, the superstitious bride can go into marriage ready for anything. She can follow all the old wives' tales and put things in her shoes and close her eyes on the way to her wedding for fear of seeing a pig or a lizard, carry a red umbrella and wear a veil. She can pray for sunshine, consult a numerologist, and avoid wearing red. Every culture has its own superstitions. There seem to be three categories for these warnings and advice: *thwarting the antics of evil spirits* attracted to the happy celebration, *luck*, and *fertility*.

keeping evil spirits away

* Guests throw rice, shoes, or something else to distract spirits from the couple.

* A veil disguises the bride so the spirits don't recognize her and make mischief.

* Bridesmaids dress alike to fool evil spirits and kidnappers, and to distract them from identifying the bride.

* The noise of cans dragging behind the getaway vehicle frightens evil spirits.

* Chinese brides carry a red umbrella to ward off bad spirits.

* The groom in Italy carries a bit of iron in his pocket as protection from *malochino*, the evil eye.

luck

Before the wedding

* It is unlucky to let another woman try on your engagement ring; she'll be the one to steal your husband.

* It is unlucky to practice writing your new name before the wedding.

* It is unlucky for the bride to practice walking down the aisle, so get a stand-in for the rehearsal.

* It is unlucky in Finland to tie knots on the wedding day until after the ceremony.

* It is lucky for the bride to put a match in her shoe to ensure the couple keep their passion burning.

* It is unlucky for the groom to see the bride in her finery until the ceremony.

On the way to the wedding

* It is unlucky for the groom to return to his house once he has begun the journey to the wedding.

* It is lucky to run into a chimney sweep or charwoman on the way, even luckier to be kissed by one.

* It is unlucky to come upon a pig, a hare, or a lizard on the way to the ceremony.

* It is lucky to come upon a lamb, a spider, or a rainbow.

* It is unlucky to see an open grave on your wedding day.

* It is unlucky to meet a nun or a monk on the way.

During your wedding

✻ It is unlucky for the bride to step into the church on her left foot.

✻ It is unlucky for the groom to drop the ring during the ceremony.

✻ It is lucky to congratulate the groom, but unlucky to congratulate the bride.

✻ It is unlucky in the Jewish and Chinese traditions to receive a knife. The bride must hand the giver a coin so it becomes a purchase, rather than a gift.

✻ It is lucky to smash the glasses after your toast to your new life, so those glasses can never be used for a better purpose.

After your wedding

✻ It is lucky for the groom to carry the bride over the threshold so she doesn't stumble when she enters her new home or accidentally make her first step on the wrong foot.

✻ A lucky couple will have one baby for every ribbon broken opening bridal shower gifts.

✻ In China it is considered lucky for the groom's parents to buy the bed for the newlyweds. Then a male relative rolls over the mattress to ensure the conception of a boy.

✻ In Scotland it was thought to be lucky for a nursing mother to make up the marriage bed, ensuring a fruitful marriage.

✻ In Ireland a laying hen was tied to the post of the honeymoon bed for luck with fertility.

fertility

* Raining the couple with grain after the ceremony is traced back to ancient Hebrews, Assyrians and Egyptians. Grain and seeds represented fertility, bounty, abundance and good fortune. These were tossed at the couple after the marriage was solemnized to bless them and their future.

* In Rome the bride carried a sheaf of wheat, or wore a crown of wheat on her head. The guests showered the couple with grains of wheat for a prosperous and fruitful marriage. Unmarried girls scooped up the grains in hopes they would be next to become a bride.

* In Italy it was popular to throw little sweets and sugar coated almonds at the bride and groom; in modern Italy it is now more often colorful *confetti* (*confetti* is Italian for "little confection").

* In Elizabethan times the wheat was baked into small cakes, which the guests crumbled over the bride's head. Eventually the cake got bigger and was eaten at the wedding celebration. Rice was an inexpensive alternative for guests to spread their blessings on the pair.

* Wheat is still the grain tossed at French wedding ceremonies.

* Throwing rice over the couple to bless them is tradition in some Asian cultures and has been an American tradition for generations.

❋ Many modern couples avoid (and many wedding venues prohibit) throwing rice. This is due to the urban myth that rice swells inside birds which causes their stomachs to burst, killing them. There is actually NO evidence of this theory being true at all. All over the world birds eat rice in nature. However, it is true that insurance companies see uncooked rice on the ground as a slip-and-fall hazard.

❋ It is popular now to throw confetti or birdseed, silk or real flower petals, sequins, autumn leaves, lavender, paper snowflakes. Often the couple is surrounded by bubbles on their way down the aisle, guests holding candles, or even lit sparklers (keep those away from that gown!)

❋ Moroccan wedding guests toss figs, dates, and raisins for a fertile joining.

❋ The Korean father of the groom throws red dates at the bride for fruitfulness.

other things we throw

* Throwing pots and pans at the newly domestic couple was an old Celtic custom.

* Some eastern Europeans toss eggs at the couple representing new life, new beginnings.

* The groom may remove his new wife's garter and toss it to the single male guests. The catcher will be the next to marry.

* The bride tosses her bouquet over her shoulder to the single female guests; the one who catches it is next to wed. Supposedly this tradition began with the throwing of her shoe.

* Druid brides carried herbs on their wedding day. After the celebration the guests would follow the couple home, continuing the reverie outside the house. In the American south this custom, called "shivaree," is still performed. It's fitting that the name of this annoying tradition comes from the Latin word for "headache." When the newlyweds tired of this foolishness, the groom lit the bouquet on fire and threw it out the door to signal it was time for them to go away.

* It was a Tudor custom for the guests to throw their shoes at the departing couple after the marriage feast. It was thought hitting their carriage sent them off with good luck. Today we tie shoes to the getaway car for the same result.

new traditions

Wedding rituals and practices evolve, and new traditions are born o
old ones come back into fashion. The old guest book sign-in is fading
away; you already have everyone's address (you mailed them an invita-
tion). Today guests can draw and write personal messages and advice
and good wishes with colored felt pens on a whole page in a scrap-
book. Decide which customs have meaning to you or your families and
feel free to create your own and encourage loved ones to embrace
them in the future. In the past few decades these new or revived cus-
toms are popular with brides:

* Wedding website
* Online gift registry
* Bachelorette parties
* No veil or no blusher
* Both parents "give away" bride
* Tussie-mussie instead of corsages for mothers
* No promise to "obey" in vows
* Unity candle ceremony
* Throwing birdseed instead of rice
* Blowing bubbles during recessional
* Photo booth at reception
* Videographer
* Photo album instead of guest book
* Honor attendant toast to groom
* Sweetheart table for just bride and groom

music

The music for your ceremony creates the atmosphere and emphasizes the emotion and significance of the moment. It keeps the guests entertained during seating and announces your arrival. Professional musicians can adapt to all your requirements, but recorded music works just as well as long as someone qualified is managing it. Imagine the flow of your ceremony while listening to a variety of music. You will find pieces that have the feeling you want. Here you will find suggestions from classical to modern.

most popular ceremony music

Whether you use live or recorded music, consider the traditional part
of the ceremony when making your selection:

> Ceremony
>
> Arrival of guests
>
> Mothers' seating
>
> Processional for attendants
>
> Processional for the bride
>
> Recessional

classic

"Bridal Chorus" (from *Lohengrin*), Richard Wagner

"Air" (from Water Music Suite), George F. Handel

"Canon in D," Johann Pachelbel

"Procession of Joy," Hal Hopson

"Rigaudon," Andre Campra

"Spring" (from *The Four Seasons*), Antonio Vivaldi

"Te Deum," Marc-Antoine Charpentier

"The Prince of Denmark's March," Jeremiah Clarke

"Trumpet Tune," Henry Purcell

"Trumpet Voluntary," Jeremiah Clarke

"Wedding March" (from *The Marriage of Figaro*),
Wolfgang Amadeus Mozart

modern

"Appalachia Waltz," Yo-Yo Ma, Edgar Meyer, Mark O'Connor

"Sunrise, Sunset" (from *Fiddler on the Roof*),
Sheldon Harnick & Jerry Bock

"The Look of Love," Dionne Warwick/Burt Bacharach

"The Vow," Jeremy Lubbock

"To A Wild Rose," Edward MacDowell

"Flatbush Waltz," Andy Statman

"Wedding Processional," (from *The Sound of Music*),
Rodgers & Hammerstein

sacred

"All People That On Earth Do Dwell" (hymn)

"Dona Nobis Pacem" (16th-century hymn)

"Hanava Babanot" (a love song), Neeman

"St. Anthony's Chorale," Franz Joseph Haydn

"Hymn Fanfare" (from the *Triumphant*), Francois Couperin

"Scalero de Oro," traditional Sephardic

"Ave Maria," Franz Schubert

Do you know the story behind the traditional processional music "Here Come the Bride?" The march is actually "The Bridal Chorus" from the opera *Lohengrin,* by Wagner. In this tragic tale, the bride, Elsa, breaks a sacred promise made to her groom on their wedding night, and he leaves her. As she watches him sail away, she dies. Still, it's a wonderful and triumphant piece of music for your entrance—well, unless you're Elsa!

the reception

flowers

music

food

favors

flowers

Flowers for the venue are a variable; some locations need more decorating than others. An outdoor ceremony in a garden may need no flower arrangements, but a plain reception hall may need embellishing with flowers, plants, or trees. You may want an arch as a focal point for the ceremony, a decorated chuppah for a Jewish wedding, or garlands and bouquets for the altar of the church. Traditionally the flowers include bouquets for the bride and her female attendants, boutonnieres for the groom, groomsmen, and fathers, flowers for mothers, coronets and petals for the flower girls, and decorations for the reception site. Bouquets for the women and the centerpieces on the tables at the reception can be simple or elaborate. But they should express your personal style and the theme of your celebration.

flowers to-do

1. Make a list of everything you would want if you had all the money in the world. Do you fantasize an arch of white orchids? How about hundreds of pink garden roses in centerpieces six feet high, lit by candelabra dripping with crystal beads? A bridal boa made of fresh flowers might be your dream. Collect pictures of flowers you like. If a friend had great bouquets or centerpieces, ask to borrow a photo and copy it. Tear out pictures of bouquets, centerpieces, and floral decorations you like from magazines.

2. Make decisions about the theme, or the "look and feel" of your event. Your dream wedding and your personal style determine the flowers. What colors do you both love? Do you want a glitzy celebrity-style glamorous event, or a Tuscan banquet set at a long table next to a vineyard? Cinderella or Zen? Do you want to carry a simple handful of herbs tied with a ribbon or a cascade of orchids and gardenias decorated with rhinestones and satin? Daytime or evening? Intimate or grand? Indoors or outside? Casual or formal? Opulent or minimalist, traditional or new age? Do you want your flowers to honor elements of family culture and religion, or to help create your own new and unique way of marrying?

3. When the date and location are secured, note which flowers will be available at that time. (*See page 106*) Orchids are always available for a Hawaiian wedding but are more costly when they are flown to the mainland. Lilacs can be had from local

growers and gardens for a few weeks in April. France and Holland export commercially grown lilacs for a longer blooming time, but you have to pay a lot more. It is easier and less expensive to use flowers that are in season.

4. List the items you will need and how many of each.

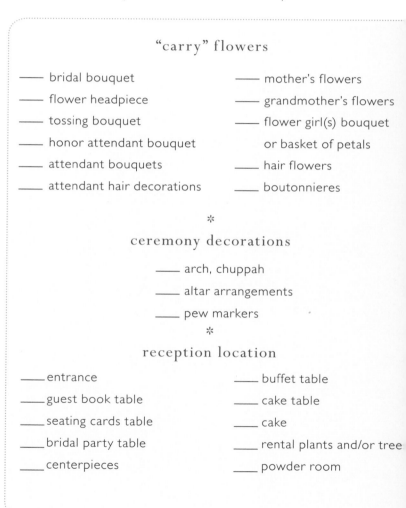

"carry" flowers

—— bridal bouquet

—— flower headpiece

—— tossing bouquet

—— honor attendant bouquet

—— attendant bouquets

—— attendant hair decorations

—— mother's flowers

—— grandmother's flowers

—— flower girl(s) bouquet
or basket of petals

—— hair flowers

—— boutonnieres

✳

ceremony decorations

—— arch, chuppah

—— altar arrangements

—— pew markers

✳

reception location

——entrance

——guest book table

—— seating cards table

—— bridal party table

—— centerpieces

—— buffet table

—— cake table

—— cake

—— rental plants and/or tree

—— powder room

5. Establish a flower budget. When you research bridal guides and wedding web sites you will read that the cost of flowers should be anywhere from 5% to 15% of your total expenditures. Flowers create the look and feel of your event and enhance everyone's enjoyment with their fragrance and beauty. Decide how much of a priority flowers are to you, and put a price on it. There are two ways to work with a florist: "Here's what I want, how much will it cost?" or "Here's what I can spend, what can you do for me?"

6. When you have picked your gown, you are ready to interview your floral designer. Make appointments with florists you already know, and anyone recommended by the coordinator, friends, and family. Bring pictures you've been collecting, lists, photos of your dress, swatches of the bridesmaids' dresses fabric, and photos of your venue or a brochure.

7. Look at the portfolios for design sensibility. If you like the work, decide if this is a person you would trust and enjoy working with. Share what you have been collecting. Tell them what you would do if money were no object. Notice if the florist gets excited about your taste and your needs and comes up with good ideas. Then tell them your budget. Ask how they envision implementing what you want with your budget. Ask the florist for a written estimate including descriptions and prices of all items, time of delivery, and a payment schedule. Have them send or email it to you.

8. When you have talked with a few floral designers, decide on which to hire. Inform your chosen florist and notify those you did not choose and thank them for their time. Get a contract and a final price in writing.

wedding flowers by season

Depending on weather conditions, the following are generally available year-round: antherium, Monte Casino aster, baby's breath, mini calla, carnation, chrysanthemum, delphinium, gardenia, Gerbera, lily-of-the-valley, hot house orchids, commercial roses, stephanotis. The following lists flowers available during certain months, many of them remain available for the whole season:

* January & February: anemone, bells of Ireland, daffodil, forget-me-not, heather, hyacinth, violet, calla lily
* March & April: allium, freesia, lilac, tulips, viburnum, muscari, ranunculus, wax flower, lily
* May & June: amaranthus, astilbe, gladiola, hydrangea, garden roses, love-in-a-mist, peony, pincushion, sweet pea, veronica, zinnia
* July & August: coreopsis, cosmos, daisy, dahlia, godetia, herbs, lavender, lisianthus, Queen Anne's lace, tuberose, sunflower
* September & October: aster, marigold, chrysanthemums, dahlia
* November & December: jasmine, poinsettia, amaryllis, holly

wedding flower meanings

The romantic Victorian Language of Flowers was a secret communication between lovers. Each bloom has been assigned meanings, and bouquets are "translated" from eighteenth-century English and French code books. The books reveal the meanings assigned to the flowers and the messages they send. You may wish to add meaning or a message to your wedding bouquet or just to know what this custom brings to the flowers you carry that day.

Alliums: *humility, unity*

Amaranthus: *immortality, unfading love, abundance*

Amaryllis: *splendid beauty, pride*

Anemone: *protective love*

Antherium: *strong attraction*

Asters: *daintiness, contentment, an afterthought*

Astilbe: *"I'll still be waiting."*

Baby's breath: *innocence*

Bells of Ireland: *good luck*

Calla lily: *magnificent beauty, elegance, ardor*

Camellia: *perfected loveliness, unabashed excellence, gratitude*

Carnation: *fascination*

Chrysanthemum, white: *absolute truth*; yellow: *"I love you,"*

Coreopsis: *gladness*

Cosmos: *modest, peaceful*

Daffodil: *regard, chivalry, returning affection, joy*

Dahlia: *dignity, forever yours*

Daisy: *innocence, simplicity, faith and cheer*

Delphinium: *light, heavenly*

Forget-me-not: *pure and true, keepsake*

Freesia: *innocence*

Gardenia: *joy, secret love*

Gerbera: *loyalty*

Gladiola: *sincerity*

Godetia: *revealing*

Heather: *passion, luck*

Holly: *foresight*

Honeysuckle: *generosity, devoted*

Hyacinth: *unobtrusive loveliness,*
unchanging youth
Hydrangea: *boastfulness,*
devotion
Jasmine: *amiability, grace*
Lavender: *devotion*
Lemon Blossom: *fidelity in love*
Lilac, white: *innocence, humility*;
purple: *first emotions of love*
Lily: *majesty*
Lily-of-the-valley: *return of*
happiness, sweetness
Lisianthus: *calming*
Love-in-a-mist: *twice kissed,*
perplexity
Marigold: *uneasiness*
Muscari: *constancy*
Orange Blossom: *purity*
and virginity
Orchid: *thoughts of you,*
ecstasy, rare beauty
Peony: *shy*
Pincushion: *unfortunate love*
Poinsettia: *mirth, good cheer*
Queen Anne's lace: *virtue,*
a haven
Ranunculus: *bedazzled, riches*

Rose: *love*
coral: *desire*
dark pink: *thankfulness*
orange: *fascination*
pale pink: *grace*
peach: *modesty, worthiness*
red: *passionate love*
white: *heavenly, innocence*
yellow: *friendship*

Stephanotis: *married bliss,*
a distant journey
Sunflowers: *adoration*
Sweet pea: *blissful delicate*
pleasure, enjoyment
Tuberose: *dangerous love*
Tulip: *declaration of love,*
perfect lover
Veronica: *fidelity*
Viburnum: *family roots,*
young beauty
Violet: *faithfulness*
Wax flower: *wealth*
Zinnia: *lasting affection, goodness*

greens

Angel vine: *intoxication*

Galyx: *long-lasting friendship*

Ivy: *wedded love, eternal fidelity*

Lemon leaf: *excitement*

Mistletoe: *rising above, surmounting difficulty*

Palm: *success*

Smilax: *lovely*

herbs

Basil: *good wishes*

Bay: *glory*

Chamomile: *comfort, gentleness*

Coriander: hidden merit

Mint: *virtue*

Oregano: *happiness, joy*

Parsley: *festivity*

Rosemary: *remembrance*

Sage: *wisdom*

Thyme: *courage, enjoyment*

The rose has been the most popular wedding bouquet flower since the Victorian era.

the bride's bouquet

Bridal bouquets can be natural, loose, and wild, tight or architectural in their shape. Hand-tied or wired, white or color or both, with embellishments and hanging ribbons or unadorned; there is a right one for you. The shape and size of the bouquet should complement the shape and coloring of the gown.

Gown style:	Suggested bouquet:
A-line / Princess:	*nosegay, round or oval with a long, wide ribbon*
Ball gown:	*a cascade, or teardrop shape, medium to large to balance the skirt*
Mermaid:	*side arm bouquet or cascade with a wide ribbon bow*
Straight sheath:	*loose, natural unstructured shape, with hanging ribbons*

bouquet shapes

Dome: *circular bouquet rounded
on top, stem handle at the bottom*

✻

Nosegay: *small round dome,
ribbon-wrapped stem handle and hanging ribbons*

✻

Biedermier: *a nosegay of concentric rings
of different flowers and leaves*

✻

Round, Oval: *flowers gathered to
form a circle or oval, handle centered behind*

✻

Heart: *wired or hand tied, heart-shaped
with ribbon-bound stem handle*

✻

Cascade: *irregular shaped bouquet,
flowers spilling downward*

✻

Side arm: *flowers arranged
to lay on the bride's crooked arm*

✻

Tussie mussie: *small bouquet of
mixed flowers in a small silver holder*

flower trivia

* In ancient times, a bride carried a handful of herbs, believed to have the power to ward off jealous and malevolent spirits and to bring her good luck and fertility.

* A Czech bride wears a crown of rosemary woven by her maid of honor.

* Some Scandinavian grooms sew herbs into their clothes for luck. This custom begat the boutonniere.

* Bay laurel leaves are scattered on the path to the church door in French weddings.

* It is an old German custom for the bride's mother to put dill and salt in her daughter's shoe.

* In some Middle East cultures artemisia, a bitter herb, is placed amongst the bridal flowers to remind her she will endure the bitter as well as the sweet in marriage. Artemisia is an ingredient in absinthe, and like wormwood and tarragon, it comes from the daisy family.

* Roman brides carried sheaves of wheat in their wedding to symbolize prosperity and fertility.

* In ancient Greece, wedding attendants wore garlands of hyacinth in their hair to honor Ceres, the goddess of agriculture. The bride wore a wreath of ivy on her head symbolizing fidelity.

* During Tudor rule in England, brides carried marigolds sprinkled with rosewater, then ate them at the wedding feast because they were believed to be aphrodisiac.

* English girls were told if they put daisies under their pillows they would dream of their true love; if they put a daisy in their bridal shoe, they would be blessed with a baby in the first year.

* In Queen Victoria's England, a bride carried a bouquet made of several smaller nosegays, which she gave to each of her brides-maids after the ceremony. One of the bunches of flowers hid a ring, and the bridesmaid who got it would be the next to marry.

* Victorian brides tucked keepsakes and sentimental trinkets into their bridal bouquet. A lock of beloved's hair, a memento of an ancestor, a photograph, or a piece of jewelry were added to the flowers and ribbon in her bouquet.

* Greek Orthodox couples wear crowns of orange blossoms, said to be the only plant that bears fruit and flowers at the same time.

* In Hawaii, the groom wears an open-ended lei of fragrant maile leaves.

* The Hawaiian bride wears many strands of crown flower, pikake, and stephanotis lei.

* Thai mothers of the bride and groom walk up the aisle and place flower garlands, *puang malai*, on their children's shoulders for good fortune in their future.

* In Hindu weddings, one of the groom's male relatives showers the couple with petals at the close of the ceremony to keep evil spirits away.

* In Polynesia, the bride walks barefoot on a path strewn with frangipani blossoms.

* Some brides carry a fan or a prayer book decorated with flowers instead of a bouquet.
* A Jamaican bride sprinkles rose petals on the train of her dress for her formal wedding portrait.
* It's an American custom to create a bouquet from the shower gift ribbons for the bride to carry at the rehearsal.
* Dutch brides carried bouquets of lily-of-the-valley. Together, the couple would plant the pips in their garden after the wedding, and the flowers bloom for their first anniversary.
* In Poland, sugar is sprinkled over the bridal bouquet to keep her sweet.
* It is customary to make the groom's boutonniere with a flower plucked from the bride's bouquet. Thus begins the sharing of everything with each other.

You may decide to do your flowers yourself. If you do, make sure you enlist some help.

* Table arrangements can be done a day ahead, but you don't want to be making boutonnieres the morning of your wedding. If you have friends and family with the crafting gene who volunteer to create your wedding flowers, accept gratefully, be in on all the planning, and keep things simple.
* Key info for florists: wedding date, expected number of guests, and number of attendants.

music

Music can be one of the most memorable and personal elements of your wedding, so you want to think carefully about the best music for every part of the event. Will you want live music or a DJ? Consider what best suits your taste and budget. You want to ensure that your guests have fun celebrating this day with you, and one of the best ways to do that is dancing at the reception.

to-do

1. Make lists with your groom of favorite songs for romance, traditions, and dancing.

2. Request a playlist from your bandleader or DJ, then make an appointment to discuss your music choices (and a Do Not Play list, too).

3. Rehearse the first dance, and time the song. You may want to cut its length.

4. Include parents in deciding the music for your dances with them.

5. Make a music list for each part of the reception:

> *Guests' arrival at reception*
> *Announcing the bride and groom*
> *Music during meal*
> *First dance*
> *Bride and father's dance*
> *Groom and mother's dance*
> *Reception dancing*
> *Last dance*

popular songs by type

～❦～

first dance

"Unchained Melody" by The Righteous Brothers

"Faithfully" by Journey

"Don''t Know Much" by Aaron Neville & Linda Ronstadt

"I Finally Found Someone" by Barbra Streisand

"Valentine" by Jim Brickman & Martina McBride

"Open Arms" by Journey

"Bless the Broken Road" by Rascal Flats

"At Last" by Etta James

"Wonderful Tonight" by Eric Clapton

"Everything I Do (I Do It for You)" by Bryan Adams

father-daughter dance

"Butterfly Kisses" by Bob Carlisle

"Because You Loved Me" by Celine Dion

"You Raise Me Up" by Josh Groban

"There You''ll Be" by Faith Hill

"The Way You Look Tonight" by Frank Sinatra

"Hero" Mariah Carey

"Dance With My Father" by Luther Vandross

"What a Wonderful World" by Louis Armstrong

"Wind Beneath My Wings" by Bette Midler

"I Will Always Love You" by Whitney Houston

mother-son dance

"What a Wonderful World" by Louis Armstrong

"Simple Man" by Lynyrd Skynyrd

"My Wish" by Rascal Flatts

"Unforgettable" by Nat King Cole

"Through the Years" by Kenny Rogers

"Stand by Me" by Ben E. King

"Because You Loved Me" by Celine Dion

"Bridge Over Troubled Water" by Simon & Garfunkel

"In My Life" by The Beatles

"Just the Way You Are" by Billy Joel

romantic

"I Will Always Love You" by Whitney Houston

"True Companion" by Marc Cohn

"At Last" by Etta James

"Total Eclipse of the Heart" by Bonnie Tyler

"Lover Lay Down" by The Dave Matthews Band

"Amazed" by Lonestar

"Wonderful Tonight" by Eric Clapton

"All I Want Is You" by U2

"My Heart Will Go On" by Celine Dion

"You"re Beautiful" by James Blunt

last dance

"Last Dance" by Donna Summer

"Remember When" by Alan Jackson

"Fantasy (Remix)" by Mariah Carey (Featuring ODB)

"You Never Can Tell" by Chuck Berry (from Pulp Fiction)

"Bless the Broken Road" by Rascal Flatts

"Wonderful Tonight" by Eric Clapton

"Where Everybody Knows Your Name"

by Gary Portnoy and Judy Hart Angelo

"The Way You Look Tonight" by Frank Sinatra)

"From This Moment On" by Diana Krall

party

"ABC" by Jackson Five

"Love Shack" by The B-52s

"Brown Eyed Girl" by Van Morrison

"Twist and Shout" by The Beatles

"We Are Family" by Sister Sledge

"I'm a Believer" by The Monkees

"Celebration" by Kool and the Gang

"Baby, I Need Your Lovin" by Four Tops

"The Locomotion" by Little Eva

"Sweet Caroline" by Neil Diamond

dancing

When there's dancing, there's joy, especially at weddings. One of the most romantic moments is when the bride and groom dance together for the first time as a married couple, swaying and gliding to what is commonly known to them forever as "our song." Once the floor opens to everyone else, the festivities really begin, with the classic celebratory dances specially reserved for weddings. Here's a small sampling:

At Cajun weddings, unmarried girls traditionally dance alone with a broom. But in Slovakia, the bride dances with a broom to welcome a happy home life.

※

The money dance is a favorite in Poland, the Philippines, and Hawaii. Guests must pay to dance with the bride and groom by pinning money to their clothing or placing it in special pouches worn by the bride and groom.

※

Dancing is a central part of Irish weddings, where guests compete in contests to do the best jig. The winner takes the cake, literally: a miniature version of the wedding cake.

Bridesmaids and single women at a Norwegian wedding will blind-fold the bride for the "crown dance," for a chance to wear the bride's gold-and-silver-bangled headdress. Once the music begins, the bride tries to capture one of her single friends and crown her. The dancing continues until all the participants have had the opportunity to wear the crown.

*

One of the most festive moments at a Jewish wedding is the cel-ebrated Horah, or chair dance. Guests hoist up chairs holding the bride and groom and dance to "Hava Nagila." At Irish weddings, the groom's best lads will lift him up in a "jaunting chair" and dance him around the room.

*

A French Canadian custom allows the bride and groom to poke fun at their unmarried older siblings during the sock dance. The single siblings wear colorful embroidered socks and take center stage while others tease them.

*

Italian brides and grooms dance the tarantella, an exotic dance that increases with speed as it nears the end, leaving everyone breathless and exhausted!

food

The food you serve is important for the enjoyment of everyone. In most weddings it is the biggest chunk of the budget. Your choices, and the quality and presentation of the meal, are critical to the success of your event. Possibilities are endless. At-home weddings may be a potluck, or cooked by the families for the whole crowd. You can order a complete Hawaiian luau including lei for everyone or a New England lobster feed, complete with bibs, all delivered from the source and served on your favorite beach. Most couples have a dinner or luncheon and hire a caterer or use the venue's chef and kitchen. Not looking for a big expensive affair? You can also consider a morning ceremony and brunch buffet or an after dinner service with desserts, liqueurs, and an espresso bar.

to-do

1. When you have your date and have booked your wedding venue you will know if they will provide the food or if they require you to use a list of caterers approved by them.

2. Make an appointment to meet with the catering manager at your location, or with catering companies on their list to discuss the menu and service.

3. If you must find a caterer yourself, investigate who did the food for any events you have attended where the food was good and well presented. Call them for an appointment.

4. Look at your guest list and note anyone you know who has food allergies or is a vegan or vegetarian, and keep this in mind when you make your selections. Do what you can to accommodate them in some way. If you and/or your groom are vegetarians it is entirely proper to serve a vegetarian meal; it's your wedding.

5. Give the caterer an estimate of the number of people you expect, and tell them what your budget is.

6. Start by telling them if you have a theme and if there are dishes you already know you want included in the menu.

7. Ask if they have experience with any ethnic dishes you want to serve.

8. Look at their portfolio; let them give you ideas and tell you about their specialties and presentations.

9. Decide whether to have a sit-down meal or buffet. Buffets usually cost less because there is less wait staff required. However

if you are having a home wedding, buffets will increase the cost of your rentals since you will need additional platters, bowls, serving utensils, and tables.

10. Offering guests a choice of entrée may be more expensive, so discuss options with your caterer. If you decide to offer a choice, it works well to offer one meat and one fish or meatless entrée. Have the choices printed on your R.S.V.P. cards for guests to check so that you can give the breakdown to the caterer in advance.

11. Agree whether the caterer will rent the tables & chairs, linens and dishes, or if you must arrange it with a rental company yourself. Determine if they can get linens that enhance your theme or color scheme. Ask if there are delivery, set-up, takedown, and cleanup charges.

12. Inquire about their tipping policy. Ordinarily it is a set percentage of the total bill, 15% to 20%, added to the bill and distributed to the staff by the caterer. You always can give additional cash tips to any individual for extra excellent service.

13. Discuss beverages and bar, wines with the meal, corkage charges if you provide the wine, and cutting charges if the cake comes from a baker.

14. At the conclusion of your caterer meetings ask them to prepare a written proposal with estimated costs and mail or email it to you. Once you have the estimates you can always work out how to adjust them to fit your budget.

15. When you are confident you have narrowed it down to a few caterers, call each and tell them you like their proposal and

want to have a tasting. Make an appointment for the two of you plus whoever else is contributing to the cost. There will be a charge, but the one you hire usually includes it in the wedding reception bill.

16. After the tastings, discuss which caterer made you feel confident, what food tasted and looked best, and who had the most value for their price. Decide which one to hire.

17. Hire the caterer, work out details, and get a firm, detailed, written contract.

18. Inform the venue manager which caterer you have engaged, and who the contact person is.

19. Arrange for leftovers to go to a homeless shelter when the celebration is over.

tipping

T.I.P.S. stands for "To Insure Prompt Service." Make sure to include tips in your budget; they can add up to a significant amount. Put checks or cash in envelopes for each person the day before the wedding. Have cash ready for extra tips. Designate someone to distribute the gratuities; often it's the best man or the wedding coordinator.

tipping guide:

* **Band:** $25 to each band member, up to $100 for the leader (it is customary to give cash for overtime)

* **Bartender:** 15% to 20% of the bar bill (put a "No tipping, please" sign on the bar—you should do the tipping, not your guests).

* **Caterer/baker:** not expected, but if the work was extraordinary, you may want to reward them with $100 or more.

* **Church musician/soloist:** $35 to $75 unless it's included in the church fee.

* **DJ:** 15% of fee

* **Driver:** 15% to 20% of the fee.

* **Florist:** not expected, but if the work was extraordinary, you may want to reward them with $100 or more.

* **Hair, makeup, manicurist:** 15% to 20% of their fee
* **Officiant:** Members of the clergy are usually not tipped; their services are included in your agreement with the church where you marry. If that is not the case, however, $75 is the least you should pay as a donation to their organization. Public officials are not permitted to accept tips. Judges usually accept a gratuity instead of a fee, at least $75. If they travel, you should also cover their expenses and may want to invite them to the reception.
* **Photographer:** not expected, but if the work was extraordinary, you may want to reward them with $100 or more.
* **Valet, coat check, parking attendants:** discretionary, these people count on tips.
* **Wait staff:** gratuity or service charge (18% to 20%) is usually included in the bill. If not, tip the wait staff 15% of the food bill, divided by the number of staff. You may want to add a cash bonus to anyone who gave particularly special service.
* **Wedding planner:** not expected, but if the work was extraordinary, you may want to reward them with $100 or more.

toasts

"To life, to health, to love," is a toasting tradition. Glasses raised, the audience agrees and clinks glasses to honor the one being toasted. The sentiment may be short, long, funny, or poetic, and custom allows a little bit of bawdiness. The toast can be about personal history with the bride and groom, good wishes, the future.

order of speakers

At a wedding reception there is an expected order of toasts, followed by anyone and everyone who wants to give one:

1. **The host:** most often the father of the bride, thanks the guests for coming, tells a memory or two about the bride, offers good wishes for the couple's future.
2. **The best man:** congratulates the newlyweds and wishes them well, tells some stories about the groom and the bride's affect on him, and jokes at the groom's expense. Last he raises his glass to the bride and toasts her and the couple's health, love, and life.
3. **The maid of honor:** congratulates the groom, tells stories about the bride, toasts to the couple's health, love, and life.
4. **The groom:** thanks the host, thanks the guests for coming to the celebration, toasts the bridesmaids.

what to say

During a wedding reception you hear spontaneous, planned, heartfelt and humorous toasts. The bride may make a request for something specific: a favorite poem or quote, something inspiring, romantic, or funny. Listed are five examples, but toasting is a long-established tradition so there are many books and online resources available to help you write your own or find the perfect sentiment.

Suggested toasts:

'Coming together is a beginning; keeping together is progress; working together is success."

'I have known many, liked not a few, loved only one. I toast to you."

'There is nothing nobler or more admirable than when two people who see eye to eye keep house as man and wife, confounding their enemies and delighting their friends."

"Let us toast the health of the bride; let us toast the health of the groom; let us toast the person that tied; let us toast every guest in the room."

"My greatest wish for the two of you is that through the years your love for each other will so deepen and grow, that years from now you will look back on this day, your wedding day, as the day you loved each other the least."

Suggested resources:

www.freeweddingtoasts.net

www.atoasttoyourwedding.com

www.weddings.about.com

www.weddingtoastsfree.com

Wedding Toasts Made Easy! The Complete Guide by Tom Haibeck

✳

Town & Country Wedding Speeches & Toasts: And other Words for Family and Friends by Caroline Tiger, Editors of *Town & Country*

✳

Wedding Toasts and Speeches: Finding the Right Words by Jo Packham

✳

Diane Warner's Complete Book of Wedding Toasts by Diane Warner

✳

Pocket Guide to Wedding Speeches and Toasts by Darren Noel

the wedding cake

Today's wedding cakes are brilliantly constructed to achieve outrageous heights, exotic shapes, and infinitely varied decorations; you can have the design any way you wish.

tradition and lore

Legend has meshed the customs of eating wedding cake and throwing grain at the couple. Grain represented fertility and abundance, hence the tossing of wheat or rice in so many cultures.

✻

In ancient Rome, we know that bread was broken over the bride's head, "breaking" her virginity and ensuring fertility.

✻

In Scotland, it is still a common ritual to crumble oatcakes on the bride. When bread, then cake, was crumbled over the bride's head, the female guests gathered the crumbs and took them home. Placed under the pillow, the crumbs would make the maiden dream of her future husband.

✻

In medieval times, the wedding feast included a stack of sweetened buns with fruit and raisins, and the newlyweds kissed above the pile. Through the 18th century in England, "Bride's Pie"—made of mince, sweetbreads, or mutton—was served after the ceremony.

to-do

The wedding cake is the centerpiece of the reception, and like the dress, it defines your theme and your personal style. You should love both the look and the taste.

1. Collect pictures of cakes you like from magazines and websites. Watch a few episodes of TV shows about creating wedding cakes.
2. Talk with your caterer. Ask if they make the cake or have favorite bakers to recommend. If they do not provide the cake, ask if they charge to cut and serve.
3. Four months before the wedding, make appointments with local bakeries and cake artists:
4. Give the baker the number of guests the cake will need to serve. Cost is calculated on a per-serving price.
5. Ask to see their portfolio; the perfect cake for you may already be in their repertoire.
6. Tell the baker what your dream cake would look like.
7. Discuss decorating options, including what will be on the top of the cake.
8. Ask if there is a delivery charge.
9. Ask what time the cake will arrive at your venue.
10. Get a description or sketch with a written estimate.
11. Make an appointment for you and your fiance to have a tasting. Choose your favorites together, but take this opportunity to give the final decision to the groom-to-be. The design is properly the bride's choice.

around the world

In America, the three-tier layer cake with white frosting and decorations is the iconic wedding cake. Today cake designers will create a cake that incorporates magical pulled-sugar flowers, faux jewels, edible ribbons, or even the lace pattern of your gown.

* *Croquembouche*, a pyramid of cream-filled profiteroles, dipped in caramel or melted sugar, is served at French wedding receptions.
* Lithuanian wedding parties have a *šakotis*, a pyramid of yellow cookie-like confections topped with fresh flowers and herbs.
* Icelanders pile almond pastries called *kransakaka* and fill the center with candies and pieces of chocolate.
* The Danish version of wedding cake is a ring made of almond cake and marzipan with candy, fruit, or sorbet in the middle, decorated with royal icing.
* In Norway, they serve *brudlaupskling*, white bread topped with cheese and soaked with cream and syrup, cut into little squares.
* In England, wedding cake is fruitcake, the top layer saved for the first baby's christening.
* Scottish and Irish wedding cakes are also fruitcake, soaked in whiskey, with almond paste between the layers.
* Jamaicans have fruitcake, too, but theirs is soaked in rum and sprinkled with rose petals.
* Korean wedding guests get cake made of ground steamed rice decorated with red bean powder.

* Chinese receptions feature a multi-tiered confection that represents the couple's ladder toward success in all they do together. They cut from the cake and personally feed pieces to each generation in their families who are present.

* In Southern China, little steamed rice cakes decorated with good fortune symbols are prepared by the bride's family and delivered along with the invitation.

* Indonesians make a *Lapis Surabaya* (Mandarin cake) or *spiku,* an unfrosted sponge cake with a yellow layer and a chocolate layer, best achieved using rich Dutch butter.

* A German wedding cake is a sponge cake with nuts, jam, and a liqueur, frosted with marzipan, fondant, or chocolate ganache.

* Italians don't always have a wedding cake, but sometimes serve the strawberry-covered *mille foglie,* made of thin pastry and chocolate cream.

* Greeks offer a flourless (therefore gluten-free) fruit and cream-filled almond cake and sourdough bread with beads and flower buds on the crust.

toppers

On the island of Bermuda, a little cedar sapling tops the cake and is planted later in the newlywed's garden to show their growing love. In the US, we tend toward tiny bride and groom statues. You may top your wedding cake with anything you want:

✳ Fresh flowers are beautiful on the cake and should coordinate with the bouquets and table decorations. The baker can get flowers from your florist or have the florist put them on the cake at the venue.

✳ A cake topper inherited from a mother or grandmother is very special. But only use if their marriage was a lasting one!

✳ Consider a vintage bride & groom topper. Browse antique stores and online auctions. I had a client whose bride & groom were on motorcycles on the top of the cake. Another had kissing frogs! At a beach wedding I coordinated, the cake had brown sugar "sand" topped with Bikini Barbie™ and Surfer Ken™.

Thanks to Queen Victoria and other royals, the craze for elaborate, multi-tiered cakes spread throughout Europe. The primary centerpiece of Queen Victoria's wedding was a plum cake that measured 3 yards in circumference and 14 inches in depth, and weighed 300 pounds! In 1923, the Viscount Lascelles and Princess Mary topped that with a royal wedding cake that stood 9 feet tall and weighed a whopping 800 pounds.

* Hearts, initials, or a monogram made of precious metal, crystal, lace, fabric, or porcelain are lasting keepsakes.

* A miniature arch, gazebo, or trellis can have a bride & groom or birds or flowers. One client's cake had a working water fountain and lights on top!

* Doves and lovebirds frequently top wedding cakes, representing the lifetime commitment of the newlyweds. In actuality, birds that mate for life are more commonly swans, flamingos, and eagles.

* Collectors should use something you treasure that represents the joining of the two of you. Some fine china brands like Wedgwood and Lenox offer cake toppers.

* If you are a Disney fan, Mickey & Minnie and Cinderella & Prince Charming toppers are available through the Disney Store.

* A music box is an original option; it can be turning and playing while you cut the cake.

* Companies like The Younique Boutique (www.tbyinc.com) will customize figurines based on photos you provide them.

cake tradition

Custom is that the bottom layer of a three-tiered cake is for the reception, the top is for the couple, the middle is for the guests to take home.

✻

The bride and groom both hold the knife and cut the first slice of cake together; it is the first task they perform together in their new marriage.

✻

Each feeds the other a bite of cake to show they will nourish and provide for each other.

✻

The top tier of the cake was traditionally fruitcake saturated with liquor to preserve it, then wrapped and stored in a tin. It is shared by the couple on their first anniversary. Today you can freeze any cake.

Approximately one-third of weddings have a buffet; one-third a sit-down dinner; the rest serve only cake.

groom's cake

In the 1600s, the groom had a cake made which he served to the bridesmaids and toasted them with wine. Sometimes the cake was saved to share with his friends when he returned from the honeymoon. This tradition was lost for a couple of centuries, but revived in the 1920s American South. The groom's cake was wildly popularized by the red velvet armadillo cake in the 1989 hit movie, Steel Magnolias.

❋ This is a gift from the bride to her groom, to say, "See, it's not *all* about me."

❋ Contrasting the wedding cake, the groom's cake is often chocolate, spice, red velvet, or other darker cake.

❋ The groom's cake is revealed to him as a surprise.

❋ Some groom's cakes are served at the reception on a table separate from the wedding cake; some are eaten after the rehearsal dinner.

❋ This cake is usually a fun—and may be a funny—creation that speaks to the groom's heritage, passion, or hobby, be it his favorite sports team or beloved car.

favors

Giving each of your guests a souvenir gift to thank them for joining the celebration is a gracious tradition. But when you shop at party stores, read bridal magazines, or browse online looking for favors, don't be surprised if you feel overwhelmed. Originally the take-home gift was a piece of the cake, then it became a box of sweets, and for a time almonds became the customary favor. Now the guests are often treated to personalized gifts that say "Thanks," and are a reminder of the wedding day celebration.

to-do

Two things to keep in mind when considering how to express your appreciation: favors made by the couple are truly meaningful, and almost anything can be personalized with your names, wedding date, or a message.

1. Decide whether to have personalized trinkets or sweets for your favors.

2. Find or create favors that reflect your theme and color scheme.

3. Party supply stores and wedding shops offer a variety of favors, and there are thousands of websites with ideas and products for consideration. If it's going to be sweets, you'll need to shop for boxes, pretty little gift bags, and personalized ribbon.

4. Buy or order your favors and supplies no less than two months before the wedding (except the edible contents, which should be assembled the day before).

5. Gather your bridesmaids and the mothers for a favors assembling party.

6. Favors may be put at each guest's place at the table, but it is a nice tradition for the newlyweds to hand them to their guests.

7. Display the favors on a table near the door, or put them in a basket and take them around the room to deliver to everyone.

8. Consider this new spin on favors that's gaining popularity: a candy bar or buffet of sweets and bags or boxes for your guests to fill with their favorites and take home with them.

ideas for favors

* Put five sugar-coated almonds in a pretty box or cloth pouch to represent five wishes for marriage—health, wealth, fertility, happiness, and longevity. Hershey will make you custom labels for their candy bars, M&M's® will print your initials or the date on their candies.

* Local specialty products like Vermont maple syrup, California olive oil or wine, and Louisiana pralines make for meaningful favors. Weddings often have inscribed wine accessories, corkscrews, stoppers, and glasses as favors.

* You may buy wineglasses for everyone and use etching crème from the craft store to apply your initials or theirs, the date, or a message.

* Personalized or labeled soaps, candles, bells, and flower seed packets are appreciated and useful.

* For a Christmas wedding, give a personalized tree ornament. I have one from a wedding I coordinated twenty years ago. Each year I think of the couple when I hang it on my Christmas tree.

international favors

At a Brazilian wedding I attended, the favors were little bundles wrapped in crepe paper and tied with ribbons. Inside there were two soft, light, sugar-dusted cookies with caramel in the middle. It melted in my mouth. The groom told me, "The bem casados (nicely or well-married) flavor represents the sweet joining and mutual support of two people together. When you taste them you will be blessed with the happiness of newlyweds."

* Holland: small blue & white porcelain figurine, often 2 shoes
* Armenia: dried fruit & nuts
* India: a metal figure of Lord Ganesh, silver coins with a deity on one side, date and name of the bride & bridegroom engraved on the other
* China: tea & cups, red envelopes of money
* Mexico: wedding cookies in a tulle bag, a fan or pieces of pottery
* Italy: sugar coated almonds in a decorated box
* France: sugar coated almonds, dragees in a pouch
* Greece: sugar coated almonds
* Switzerland: red handkerchiefs
* Malaysia: painted hard-boiled eggs
* Japan: Kōhaku, pairs of little bean paste filled buns, one white one, red, and sometimes a decorative envelope of cash. Japanese brides make one thousand origami cranes for luck and hand them out to their guests at the end of the celebration.

welcome baskets

Welcome out-of-towners to your celebration by creating a gift basket. Arrange to deliver it to their hotel before they arrive. Every guest at a destination wedding should receive one.

Contents:

printed itinerary with phone numbers, dress, time, location, and directions for each wedding event and activity ✲ maps and brochures about nearby attractions ✲ snacks and local specialty products

for a "relax basket" add

bottle of wine (and corkscrew and 2 glasses) ✲ candles chocolate ✲ music on CD

a "sun basket" for a warm location or tropical destination, add

bottled water ✲ sunscreen ✲ lip balm ✲ aspirin disposable camera ✲ fan and sun hat

---

Chelsea Clinton's welcome gift bags had local wine from Clinton Vineyards (no relation), chocolates, locally baked pastries, and Fresh Sugar lip balm.

tradition and lore

Ancient Romans believed any object touched by the bride and groom would always be lucky. It became the custom for the couple to personally hand the favors to every guest.

✳

Twelve hundred years later in Italy, aristocrats were giving expensive parting gifts to wedding guests to thank them for attending, and to demonstrate their wealth.

✳

European nobility sometimes gave their wedding guests gifts of myrrh and incense. Also gifted were small decorative boxes known as bonbonniere, made of carved wood, painted porcelain, cut crystal, or precious metals and jewels. If given by the very wealthy, they contained elaborate confections or cubes of sugar.

✳

In Elizabethan England, the bride and groom handed out little bundles of flowers and herbs to the departing guests.

At the 1896 wedding of King Victor Emanuel and Queen Elena of Italy, all eighteen hundred guests were given solid silver figurines. At smaller Italian weddings a little gold cardboard box with five almonds inside is given to each guest to take home.

✻

Candy-coated almonds are still the customary wedding favor in the Americas, the Mediterranean, and many Middle Eastern countries. An uneven number of candies are given because they can't be divided equally, symbolizing unity.

✻

During the Renaissance, as the precious commodity sugar became more readily available in Europe, the sugar-coated almond, or *confetti*, was created. In the 14th century, the fashion was to hand out almonds at the end of a wedding, and sometimes a small piece of the cake, signifying the bitter and the sweet of married life.

the honeymoon

the honeymoon

The term "honeymoon" is Old English, from the days when men ventured to another village to capture (or escort) a bride back to his home. The couple stayed in hiding before the wedding and for a month (one cycle of the moon) afterward. They had little to do but drink mead (honey wine) and make love.

to-do

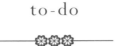

1. Make plans and reservations early so you can focus entirely on the wedding.
2. Get a passport, or renew yours if needed.
3. Research expected weather to help you make wardrobe decisions.
4. Finish packing one week before the wedding, and put the suit-cases out of sight.
5. Put someone in charge of both bride and groom's luggage and ride to airport.
6. Pack a carry-on bag with all your medications, toothbrush & paste, sunscreen, insect repellent, camera, nightgown and either a warm coat or bathing suit. This way you're covered the first day and night if your luggage is lost.
7. Balance relaxation and activities.

The first night of the honeymoon may be spent sleeping. It is reported that more than half of couples don't make love on their wedding night. They are too tired!

where to go?

✽✽✽

most popular destinations

Hawaii ✽ Bahamas ✽ Cayman Islands ✽ Jamaica
Aruba ✽ US Virgin Islands ✽ Mexico ✽ St. Marten
Europe ✽ Puerto Rico ✽ Bermuda

most popular US destinations

Hawaii ✽ New York City ✽ San Francisco ✽ Miami
Las Vegas ✽ New Orleans ✽ Aspen ✽ Lake Tahoe
Martha's Vineyard ✽ Napa Valley

when to travel

❀❀❀

You're not locked in to taking your honeymoon immediately after the wedding. If you marry in April but can't get away until August, let your honeymoon plans fit your schedule. Here are some suggestions for great destinations and the ideal time to visit them.

* January & February: Arizona, Belize, Caribbean, New Zealand
* March & April: Australia, Las Vegas, South America
* May & June: Canada, Greece, Italy, Morocco
* July & August: Alaska, Barbados, Iceland, Tahiti
* September & October: New England, Fiji, France, Spain, Napa Valley
* November & December: Asia, Costa Rica, Maldives, Mexico

The most popular honeymoon destination is Las Vegas; next most popular are nearly all tropical island destinations.

romantic honeymoon dinner

——— ❁❁❁ ———

Throughout history, certain foods have been believed to stimulate the libido because of their suggestive shapes, texture, or nutritional content. Second-century Roman satirist Juvenal was the first to note the amorous nature of women after consuming large quantities of wine and "giant oysters." Another powerful sexual stimulant is chocolate, which the Aztecs relished as the "nourishment of the gods." In the towns of France, eating strawberries is still considered to be an extremely potent way for newlyweds to nourish their libido. Create the mood for romance by setting a candlelit table for two. Then stir up some passion with this aphrodisiac-laden menu:

Appetizer

Champagne oysters with potato cakes

Entrée
Lobster & linguine with tomato-basil sauce

Dessert

Chocolate-dipped strawberries

by the numbers

————❀❀❀————

99% of newlyweds take a honeymoon.
Honeymoons usually last 7 to 9 days.
Honeymoons are a $12 billion a year industry.
Average honeymoon budget is $3,997;
three times more than a regular vacation.
43% of honeymooners will travel within the United States;
about 57% will travel to a foreign country.

transportation

3 out of 4 couples fly to their honeymoon destination
2 out of 3 rent cars
1 out of 4 goes on a boat or ship
1 out of 7 takes their own car
1 out of 35 travel by train

most popular activities:

75% Sightseeing, entertainment, restaurants and nightlife
45% Beach, water activities and water sports
20% Casinos
15% Cruises
10% Golf
5% Skiing

ways to save

———❊❊❊———

1. A honeymoon registry will cut down on costs by letting your guests gift some parts of your trip, whether it's a night at the hotel, a dinner, or a surfing lesson.

2. Honeymooning during the off-season cuts down on travel and accommodation costs.

3. Apartment/house swapping is a great way to see a city and save at the same time. Check out sites like www.couchsurfing.org to find a couple you'd be comfortable exchanging residences with.

4. All-inclusive resorts help keep down the sometimes unexpected costs that go along with regular activities—like eating and drinking.

5. The cost of a cruise is all-inclusive, and you travel with you hotel room, unpacking just once.

6. Decide on how much you can spend before you start planning. If you set a firm budget and stick to it, you'll be better prepared when it comes to deciding where to go, and when.

7. If flying to your destination, look into smaller, low-cost carriers to save on travel expense.

honeymoon registry

Like online gift registries, an online honeymoon registry allows your guests to contribute to individual elements of your ideal honeymoon. From entertainment and activities, to dining, transportation, and accommodation, your guests can help make your getaway more affordable. Some sites can charge the couple, the guests, or both for this service, and others don't, so take the time to review them and find one that's right for you. Below are a few sites to explore:

www.travelersjoy.com ✳ www.thebigday.com
www.sendusoff.com ✳ www.honeymoonwishes.com
www.honeyluna.com

tradition and lore

After all the hectic preparations for the Big Day, many couples today opt for a few peaceful, relaxing weeks in sunny seclusion. But honeymoons haven't always been languorous and restful.

The Irish translation for honeymoon is *mi na meala*, which means "the month of honey." This stems from the ancient Germanic tribal custom of the newlyweds' drinking mead, which is made from honey—to prepare for the bitter and sweet of marriage—every day for a full cycle of the moon.

⁂

In Japan, it was customary for the groom to prepare for the honeymoon by overseeing the installation of the bridal bed the day before the wedding. A "good luck woman" or a "good luck man"—someone with many children—was selected to install the newly purchased bed. Once in place, children were invited onto the bed as an omen of fertility. The bed was scattered with red dates, oranges, lotus seeds, peanuts, pomegranates, and other fruits for the same reason.

⁂

In Bulgaria the bride and groom disappear for a week to spend their first days as husband and wife in seclusion. The bride then makes a visit to the village well, accompanied by a group of married women. She circles the well three times and kisses the hands of all of the women who have come with her. The women then present her with figs to wish her a fruitful and happy life.

That romantic moment when the groom carries his bride over the threshold isn't just a display of gallantry; it's an ancient homage to the protector of the hearth and home.

The virgin Roman goddess Vespa considered the threshold sacred. Ancient Roman grooms therefore carried out this symbolic gesture to avoid letting their virgin brides touch the threshold and thereby risk being disrespectful to the goddess.

✳

In South Africa, to symbolize the fire of a new family's hearth, both sets of parents bring fire from their homes to light the first fire in the bride and groom's new home.

✳

The chimney was a traditional passageway for unwanted spirits to enter the home. Upon their initial entry, Russian couples burn straw in the hearth to smoke out any demons that might be hiding in the flue.

✳

In Greece, the bride's mother meets the bride at the door of the newlyweds' home. The mother gives the new bride a drink of honey and water so that her words will always be sweet. She then uses the rest of the drink to paint the threshold, so that their home remains a place of sweetness and peace.

the international language

———— ❀❀❀ ————

It's a very good practice to say "I love you" to your spouse every day.
For variety, here's a list of ways for newlyweds to proclaim "I love you"
in forty-six languages!

Afrikaans: *Ek het jou life*

Armenian: *Yes kez sirumen*

Bulgarian: *Obicham te*

Cambodian: *Soro lahn nhee ah*

Cantonese: *Ngo oiy ney a*

Cherokee: *Tsi ge yu i*

Czech: *Miluji te*

Danish: *Jeg Elsker Dig*

Dutch: *Ik hou van jou*

Ethiopian: *Ma armastan sind*

Farsi: *Doset daram*

Filipino: *Mahal kita*

French: *Je t'aime*

German: *Ich liebe dich*

Greek: *S'agapo*

Hawai'ian: *Aloha au ia'oe*

Hindi: *Hum tumhe pyar karte hae*

Hopi: *Nu' umi unangwa 'ta*

Hungarian: *Szeretlek*

Icelandic: *Eg elska tig*

Indonesian: *Saya cinta padamu*

Inuit: *Negligevapse*

Irish: *Taim i' ngra leat*

Italian: *Ti amo*

Japanese: *Aishiteru*

Korean: *Sarang heyo*

Lebanese: *Bahibak*

Lithuanian: *Tave myliu*

Mandarin: *Wo ai ni*

Moroccan: *Ana moajaba bik*

Navaho: *Ayor anosh' ni*

Norwegian: *Jeg elsker deg*

Persian: *Doo-set daaram*

Polish: *Kacham ciebie*

Portuguese: *Et tea mo*

Russian: *Ya tebya liubliu*

Sioux: *Techihhila*

Slovenian: *Ljubim te*

Spanish: *Te quiero*

Swedish: *Jag alskar dig*

Taiwanese: *Wag a ei li*

Tahitian: *Ua here vau ia oe*

Turkish: *Seni seviyorum*

Ukranian: *Ya tebe kahayu*

Welsh: *'Rwy'n dy garu di*

Yiddish: *Ikh hob dikh*

anniversary

———— ✿✿✿ ————

It's never too soon to start looking ahead! Each year married couples rekindle the romance and memories of their special day. Below is a list of traditional and contemporary gifts.

Year:	Traditional:	Contemporary:
1	Paper	Clocks
2	Cotton	China
3	Leather	Crystal
4	Linen	Electrical appliances
5	Wood	Silverware
6	Iron	Wood
7	Wool, Copper, Brass	Desk sets
8	Bronze	Linen, Lace
9	Pottery	Leather
10	Tin, Aluminum	Diamond jewelry
11	Steel	Fashion jewelry
12	Silk	Pearls
13	Lace	Textiles, Fur
14	Ivory	Gold Jewelry
15	Crystal	Watches
20	China	Platinum
25	Silver	Sterling Silver
30	Pearls	Diamonds
35	Coral	Jade
40	Rubies	Garnets
45	Sapphires	Tourmalines
50	Gold	Gold

Song of the Open Road

Afoot and lighthearted, take to the
    open road,
Healthy, free, the world before you,
The long brown path before you
    leading wherever you choose.

Say only to one another:
Camerado, I give you my hand!
I give you my love more precious
    than money,
I give you myself before preaching or law:

Will you give me yourself? Will you
    come travel with me?
Shall we stick by each other as long
    as we live?

—Walt Whitman